MW00436449

# Zodiac Cats

## Astrology for Our Feline Friends

# Zodiac Cats

## Astrology for Our Feline Friends

### Helen Hope

GRAMERCY BOOKS
NEW YORK

This 2007 edition is published by Gramercy Books, an imprint of Random House Value Publishing, by arrangement with Ulysses Press. Originally published by Ulysses Press under the title *Star Cats*.

Gramercy is a registered trademark and the colophon is a trademark of Random House, Inc.

Random House

New York • Toronto • London • Sydney • Auckland

www.valuebooks.com

A catalog record for this title is available from the Library of Congress.

ISBN: 978-0-517-23034-3

Printed and bound in China.

10 9 8 7 6 5 4 3 2 1

# CONTENTS

# INTRODUCTION

The feline family, especially *Catus domesticus*, has long embodied magic, mystery and fascination for *Homo sapiens*, the human species that, whether black, yellow, white or whatever, presently dominates planet Earth. (Sadly, modern-day humans failed to live up to their name—*sapiens* is Latin for wise—when they persecuted the cat in the Europe of the Middle Ages!) The lion, *Felis leo*, is still known as the "king of the jungle" and revered for its royal ways. In earlier cultures, including ancient Egypt, wearing a lion skin conferred exalted power and was reserved for the ruling elite, such as the Pharaoh or shaman. The tiger, *Felis tigris*, is still accorded the respect it has commanded through the ages for its physical majesty, its spiritual power, and its mastery of the night.

Only the cat has chosen to link its destiny as a species with humans. Cats provide us with rat control and so forth but also with the special quality of their company. I sorely felt the lack of feline inspiration and companionship when I moved to a suburb in Sydney's northern beaches some years ago. So upon hearing of a pet shop in nearby Newport, I set off at once and soon found myself up a little side street feeling as if I had wandered into the twilight zone or had stepped into another whimsical, yet mysterious, reality.

There stood two shops. One of these was filled with wall-to-wall shelves overflowing with ancient books and untold piles more on the dusty floor. A lack of lighting made it seem that there was no back wall, only a great vortex into the universe. Obviously not the pet shop.

Turning my attention to the other one, I noticed a little handwritten sign on the window, "Tarot reader within. 70 years experience." Taking a deep breath, I entered the premises, where I was met by a gentleman of quite ethereal appearance. He was of venerable age, slight and with skin like porcelain. His eyes were utterly remarkable—I have never seen the like since. The whites were the purest white, and the irises were the radiant but delicate blue of a thrush's egg. His greeting was gracious, and upon learning of my mission, he pointed me to a wire enclosure in which six newly arrived kittens were resting. They, of course, were all lovely, but the gentle and wise proprietor directed my attention to the little ginger female curled up in the front. Marmalade males were not uncommon, he told me, but a female was a rarity. And, he cautioned, sometimes they did not live past kittenhood. At that point the kitten opened her eyes, and as the blast of her blue gaze met my eyes, I knew she was coming home with me.

My little ginger puss was a Capricorn with Gemini rising. Her loyal Capricorn ways warmed my days and kept me organized. Her Gemini personality made for good communication and also helped her plot clever strategies. From the beginning she was special and, yes, I did have to coax her through frail kitten days. But she was not named Sekhmet (after the lion-headed aspect of Bastet, the great Egyptian cat goddess) for nothing. She survived well into adulthood, bringing me much enlightenment and joy through her most extraordinary being and remarkable intelligence.

Sekhmet knew everything that was going on, and often tried to warn me if I was heading in an adverse direction. For example, once when I was on the brink of packing up and moving based on emotional and irrational reasoning, she contravened all edicts by walking into my bedroom late one night and directing a flood of loud meowing at me, emphatically swishing her tail. I instantly picked up what she meant. Among other examples of her prescience, Sekhmet shunned anyone she deemed didn't have my best interests at heart. And she would often come into my study or look through the window, where she had a better vantage point, to make sure I was getting on with my work. But the best times of all were when we could sit together under the stars on the balcony or in the garden and just enjoy the whole mystery of life and our cat–person relationship within its magnificent tapestry.

And now, dear reader, I know your puss is every bit as wonderful and marvelous to you. So please read on to comprehend more of the secrets and soul of your special companion. This book is dedicated to all the cats in the world. Their ability to fascinate us, it is said, is so they can inspire and "educate" us.

# ATTRIBUTES

If you don't know your cat's date of birth, for whatever reason, read through the following chart to see which star tribe your pet's personality and habitual behavior correspond with.

**KEY**

SIGN ●

KEY WORDS ○

ATTRIBUTES ◌

## ARIES

courageous; enthusiastic; independent; impulsive; impatient; headstrong; selfish; aggressive

forceful, fiery, dynamic character; high energy; risk-taker; rebellious; not cuddly; scratches vets; enjoys playing with humans; loves fights; robust constitution

loyal; trustworthy; reliable; persevering; possessive; lazy; compassionate; stubborn

affectionate; peaceful; shy with strangers; likes children but explodes if annoyed; loves sleep and comfort; eager to please; loves routine; loathes change; melodious voice

## TAURUS

**GEMINI**

friendly; versatile; perceptive; restless; contradictory; critical; eloquent; impatient; vocal

alert; loves to be talked to; inquisitive; busy; fun-loving; enjoys people; not demonstrative; highly strung; thrives on a varied diet

sympathetic; protective; moody; industrious; sociable; sensitive; argumentative; emotional; psychic

thrives on affection; cheers people up; sits at owner's feet; sleeps with owner's sock; can be loony and jealous; loves to lick; great parent

**CANCER**

regal; optimistic; affectionate; self-centered; indolent; devoted; sunny nature; demanding; domineering; generous; enthusiastic

**LEO**

proud, fiery and competitive; meows a lot; can be sly; holds grudges; dislikes strangers in home; loves sunset or sunrise walks; good at tricks finicky; considerate; aloof; intelligent; busy; self-absorbed; systematic; reliable; industrious; shy; faithful

dedicated to serving; attention to detail; well-groomed; enjoys routine; rarely demonstrative; prefers quiet life; senses if something is amiss; soft-hearted; curious; fussy eater

**VIRGO**

cooperative; sociable; indecisive; lazy; diplomatic; helpful; vocal; dependent; eager

popular; stylish; loves being seen with owner; unpredictable; has sweet tooth; prefers leisure and companionship to work; occasionally prone to foolish behavior

**LIBRA**

**SCORPIO**

brave; resourceful; ambitious; intuitive; obstinate; determined; jealous; vengeful; efficient

"command" presence—rarely has to fight; hard to "read"; forms strong bonds with owner; nurses hurts; non-conformist; protective of children; hardy

fun-loving; makes people laugh; a charming wanderer; loathes being tied down; loves showing off; exuberant; contemplative; can seem human; enjoys music; easily side-tracked

cheerful; versatile; friendly; quarrelsome; boastful; engaging; irresponsible; loud; charismatic

**SAGITTARIUS**

patient; responsible; goal-driven; intolerant; sensible; suspicious; capable; practical; clever; reliable

takes relationship with owner seriously; avoids risk; cool in a crisis; purposeful; great zest for life; fabulous recall; undemanding; needs to feel wanted

**CAPRICORN**

social;
intuitive;
unpredictable;
inventive; rebellious;
intelligent; helpful;
independent; single-
minded

rugged
individualist; life is
a continual experiment;
freedom-loving; not cuddly;
easily bored; cheers up owner;
hearty appetites; befriends all
types of humans and
creatures

**AQUARIUS**

**PISCES**

psychic;
sympathetic;
indecisive; changeable;
hypersensitive;
impressionable; devoted;
enchanting

dependent
on owner's love; has
big highs and lows;
gentle and intuitive; flees
when stressed; adores the
outdoors; enjoys
watching TV

# ARIES *cat*

21 March–20 April

KITTY LITTER

**herb:** Rosemary

**stone:** Ruby

**number:** 9

**element:** Fire—at heart is a hunter

**celebrity cat:** Jock—who attended War Cabinet meetings with Sir Winston Churchill

ARIES CATS ARE PRETTY **PHYSICAL** ALL AROUND. THEY LOVE TO GET OUTSIDE AND STALK THINGS THROUGH THE GRASS. BIRDS HOLD RIGHTEOUS FEAR OF THEM AND WILL FLIT FAST WHEN THEY SEE YOUR PET COMING. THEY KNOW YOUR PUSS IS LETHAL AND HAS NO MERCY. OTHER CATS CAN RESPOND TO YOUR **FEARLESS** FELINE IN THE SAME WAY, TOO. BECAUSE ARIES CATS ARE **COMPETITIVE** AND **COMBATIVE** BY NATURE, AS WELL AS EASILY ANGERED, ANY CAT CHALLENGING OR CREEPING INTO THEIR TERRITORY LEARNS FAST NOT TO DO IT AGAIN.

**T**he Aries cat is ruled by Mars, god of war, courage and initiative. When this kitty's owner calls, it usually responds rather rapidly (unless caught up in combat zones, of course, or if it has other pressing matters to attend to) because this pet loves positive action. However, if you disappoint your Aries cat too often (if you don't give it enough love, admiration or goodies), then it will just stop turning up.

It's excellent that you're so interested in your feline's forceful, dynamic and charismatic character—not that it would understand if you were otherwise; this star creature regards itself as "the best cat on the planet!"—and that you wish to find out more. It sees itself as extremely interesting and does have strong needs. Your Aries puss thinks it really is best that you know of these things so that you can give it the love and care it feels entitled to, and get full enjoyment of its great personality in return. That way **all** will enjoy life a lot more.

This member of the cat star tribes has a great deal of energy. Aries kittens almost drive their owners crazy with their escapades—getting stuck up trees or on the roof, jazzing about all over the house like little tornados. Even as adults they remain risk takers and super-turbo-charged creatures. They just have a little more experience behind them.

The Aries cat is extremely independent, can **hate** being told what to do, and can be quite rebellious. Hence it may be the devil's own job to discipline it on the matter of kitty litter. (Little Aries felines tend to love getting into it, playing war and excavating, and then might be quite put out that you didn't seem to appreciate their activities!) These character traits can require a lot of forbearance and forgiveness on the part of their "humans." (Aries cats don't much like to think of you as their "owner." They leave that attitude to what they consider more "servile creatures like Cancer cats." They prefer to think of you as the "person" in their life.) However, when they do get the message and are over their dislike of details, Aries felines become—eventually—pretty responsible in that department.

This star cat has a strong sense of its own purpose. It sees it as fortunate that you are together as pet and owner but it doesn't derive its central meaning from you. Aries cat star tribe members usually have full-on lives of their own and don't have a great need for coddling and petting. In fact, they can get a bit frantic if held against their will. (You, dear owner, probably still recall how your feline nearly ripped the car to shreds on the first trip to the vet— memo to those with an Aries kitten: purchase a cat carrier immediately!) That is why it's not a good thing when a little person wants to treat an Aries cat like a cute, cuddly soft toy. (Their Pisces cousins may submit to being dressed up, but **never** Aries star cats.) Nothing is worse than an attempt at sustained holding for this freedom-loving feline. Being impetuous, impulsive and impatient, an Aries puss will scratch its way out if necessary. ("Act first, think later" can often seem to be your cat's motto!) It's not that it's a nasty and horrible cat, it's simply that its fiery, independent nature cannot take restraint in any form. And teasing an Aries cat can be really **dangerous**. The way your cat sees it is: "Play, yes; tease, no!"

Catus aries enjoy physical interaction with the people in their lives. Unlike other cats, they will often run around with humans. They like and will play definite games. Aries cats prefer life to be stimulating and full of action, so they're usually quick to pick up on the promise of something interesting. But if Aries pusses get bored, it's difficult to recapture their interest. For this star feline, when something's finished, it's finished!

Aries cats are pretty "physical" all around. They love to go outside and stalk things through the grass. Birds hold righteous fear of them and will flit fast when they see your pet coming. They know your puss is lethal and has no mercy. Other cats can respond to your fearless feline in the same way, too. Because Aries cats are competitive and combative by nature, as well as easily angered, any cat challenging or creeping into their territory learns fast not to do it again. Aries kitties full-bloodedly make short work of such "upstarts." Their claws and teeth are highly efficient, plus their bodies are usually quite powerful. This breed of star puss can be the "Rambo" of cats.

Your cat's instinctive urge is to be the dominant animal (it can even try to boss **you** in its not-so-subtle way!), and because of this Aries pusses are sometimes known to go out on the prowl and look for "physical engagement"—otherwise known as fights. Plus they've been known to give the household dog a hard time!

Your star cat's constitution is generally strong and resilient. An Aries feline is not normally an ailing one; its impulsive nature is much more likely to get it into trouble than sickly tendencies. (Many's the Aries cat that the fire brigade has had to save at least once!) Aries kitties are robust and ready to tackle life on any level they can. Your energetic puss enjoys life in a very active way.

With their positive and optimistic outlook Aries cats view themselves as "winners." Your pet assumes you know that because it's with **you**! "How's that for right choice?" it'd like to exclaim. Your star feline realizes that at times it can appear to be selfish, detached and not interested in you and your world at all; that it may seem to have no interest in your relationship as cat and person. But that is not true. It just looks that way because its life gets so busy and interesting. Your star cat would readily admit to its own desires and lust for life being fairly demanding, but would then ask: "What about those times when I rub up against your legs and there is **no** food involved?" Of course, that's when they are showing you their powerful love for you and indicating their depth of feeling for you.

And think about those times when your puss looks at you and its eyes crinkle, close, then open, telegraphing happiness and love to you. Yes. It's true. That **is** what it's doing. In fact, many of the reflections you've had about your cat's **thoughts** have been true! You have a powerful star member of the cat family, and it loves **you** fiercely.

### PAWNOTES

No doubt about it. Your cat has an extremely strong personality (probably because one of the Aries cat's heydays was while at the call of Montu, the ancient Egyptian military god honored by the army). Also not in question are the times when this puss has pushed your patience to the limits, only to be followed by periods when you are inspired by what you see in this feline of yours. (There is more and more of the latter as your pet increases in years.) Aries cats generally need fresh red meat in their diet for all-around well-being, so make sure to include some at least once a week.

# TAURUS *cat*

21 April—20 May

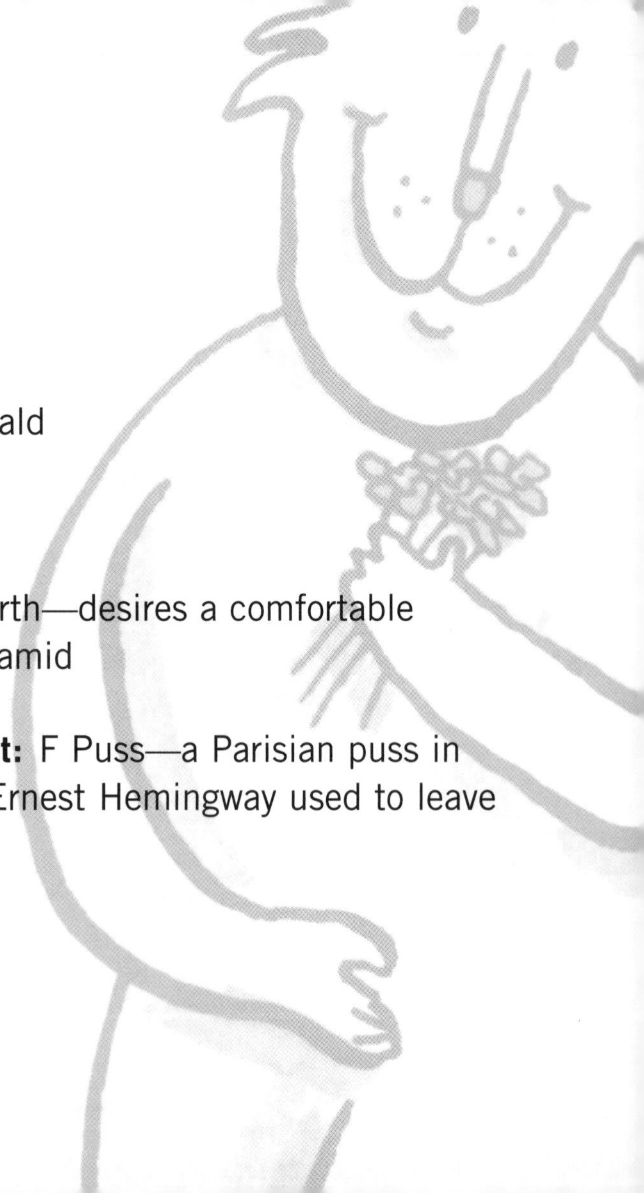

**herb:** Mint

**stone:** Emerald

**number:** 6

**element:** Earth—desires a comfortable Egyptian pyramid

**celebrity cat:** F Puss—a Parisian puss in whose care Ernest Hemingway used to leave his baby son

IF IT DOESN'T HAVE ITS OWN COMFY BASKET, THEN THIS STAR CAT WILL HAVE STAKED OUT ITS OWN SPECIAL PLACES. IT IS OFTEN TO BE FOUND CURLED IN FRONT OF THE FIRE OR STRETCHED OUT IN THE SUN, OR VICE VERSA. THIS KITTY LOVES TO SLEEP, PARTICULARLY WHEN IT CAN SNOOZE IN TOTAL **CONTENTMENT**, WITHOUT A CARE IN THE WORLD. AND WATCH IT WAKING UP! STRETCHING AND YAWNING, **PLEASURABLY** AND **LOVE-FILLED**, BACK INTO LIFE. THE TAUREAN FELINE IS GREAT TO CUDDLE AS IT TRANSITS THE STAGE BETWEEN SLEEP AND WAKEFULNESS.

**T**he Taurus cat is ruled by Venus, goddess of love, pleasure and harmony. When this feline is called, it reliably appears because it figures you've got something nice in mind, plus it also wants to see you.

Your pet would like to thank you for wanting to find out more about it. The rapport between you is pretty good, but your feline is glad that there is this opportunity to make certain things clearer. Like, for example, how profoundly it loves you, how important good food and comfort are to it, and how upsetting it finds it if daily life gets interrupted for any reason. (These matters will be elaborated on a little later.) But right now your star cat wants you to know how much it appreciates your endeavor to deepen your understanding of it. In your cat's words: "This can only work to improve the quality of the life we have together."

Taurean kitties' love for their owner is an important force in their lives. They can be possessive whenever there's **any** sign of rivalry for your affections. This possessiveness can extend to making you feel guilty about moving when it's firmly ensconced on your warm lap. This star cat adores to be patted and scratched under the chin, behind the ears and the like. Its passive force works quite well here, too. Again you feel a little uncomfortable about stopping when your puss' purring is full-throated and it is obviously in ecstasy. "However," your cat notes, "you do stop, despite my secret (not so secret now) psychic maneuvers." And then continues, "But with my love for you so strong and deep, it's only natural that I want you **all** to myself. When I can't be close to you, then I focus, get comfortable and regard you sphinx-like from a cosmically blissed-out state. It's OK when I do this, I'm just transmitting more Venus energy into our environment."

Comfort. Now that's important to the Taurus feline. If it doesn't have its own comfy basket, then this star cat will have staked out its own special places. It is often found curled in front of the fire or stretched out in the sun, or vice versa. This kitty loves to sleep, particularly when it can snooze in total contentment, without a care in the world. And watch it waking up! Stretching and yawning, pleasurably and love-filled, back into life. The Taurean feline is great to cuddle as it transits the stage between sleep and wakefulness. You can **feel** all the sheer love energy that Catus taurus has collected in its astral wanderings.

Food more or less goes with comfort, but for clarification, your cat wants me to treat it separately here. This star cat enjoys good food and lots of it! Your pet adds: "I'm not a 'garbage guts.' If I have a choice I go for quality. However, if I don't then I usually accept what's given. I like milk, too, and when I can get some I **love** cream." Taurus cats usually become plump and cuddly, with thick coats and affectionate natures, because of the energy they devote to what they refer to as "the practical side of life"—namely food and sleep.

Catus taurus has trouble coping with any radical disturbance to its environment. This is a cat that is usually in rhythm with the routines of the household, the sort of cat that will wait for you by the mailbox (if it's not too cold at the time) to come home. So even a small change in your daily patterns can disturb its peace of mind. However, Taurus cats are capable of making adjustments— eventually—particularly if you try and explain things to your puss in some way. Your cat wishes to add, "Perhaps you **should** do this when it's a major change, as I'm the type of cat that will travel back to the house we left, or pine when someone is suddenly absent."

When all is well with the world this is usually a placid and gentle star cat. Taurus kitties can be tolerant with children and not as quick to scratch as some of their brother or sister star cats. However, when small people are around, especially if their activities are of a teasing nature, do watch what is going on, as your feline's anger can steadily build. While the kids merrily go on with their teasing, thinking that this cat will put up with any indignity, Catus taurus will suddenly react with the force of an earthquake. Anyone on the scene can get scratched and will receive more than quite a fright. It's not that your cat is malicious, it is just that when it reaches a certain point, it's truly had enough. In reality, Taurus kitty is a kind animal. Provided it is with children whose intentions are good and they are not hurting your pet, this star cat can have great patience.

This cat likes a garden. The Taurus feline is not that happy if it has no natural space in which to ramble outside. And it is often observed sitting communing with nature. At other times a Taurus feline will take its time and stroll around investigating the estate. The Taurus cat has all the usual reactions to birds, mice and so on, but when it's well fed, it's really not **that** intense about it. If this puss is happy, it's usually quite content to have other living creatures around. This is definitely not one of those cats that has to kill everything in sight. This is also a cat that's unlikely to wander when its heart is in its home.

Your cat wants to have a say now: "I can seem a little shy with grown-up strangers, but it's more my natural caution at work. I like to check new people out and wait until I feel safe with them before making great overtures of friendship. I have fine vocals when I get going. My melodious voice with its magnificent range and tone (I don't **always** exercise it in front of the fridge) is something I'm very proud of. I think it's true to say that all in all I'm a good cat to have around."

Your pet is absolutely right. Taurus cats are splendid to
have around. They are sane, balanced and loving. Their
lineage goes back to Bastet, the ancient Egyptian goddess
in cat form, who embodied these qualities. These
characteristics will be more so if you take care that your
star puss feels secure. Steady affection and reliable
mealtimes are the main ingredients in this. But do watch
that your feline does not overfeed because too much rich
food will collect as fat around the organs. Also, be ready
for reactions if putting a new collar on your kitty—the
neck can be a sensitive region. A happy and content
Taurus cat is a very cuddly puss, one that's able to
magnetize more love into the atmosphere.

# GEMINI *cat*

21 May–21 June

**herb:** Parsley

**stone:** Crystal

**number:** 5

**element:** Air—can outdazzle the stars

**celebrity cat:** William (Willamina)—Charles Dickens' cat, renamed after giving birth to kittens!

NEXT TIME YOUR PET'S CLEAR, INTELLIGENT EYES ARE ENGAGED WITH YOURS, TAKE A GOOD LOOK AND YOU'LL SEE THE **REGARD** AND **LOVE** IT HOLDS FOR YOU. THE GEMINI PUSS CAN ENJOY BEING TALKED TO AS WELL. IT LIKES THE SOUND OF YOUR VOICE AND SOMETIMES IT'LL TALK BACK! THIS IS A HIGHLY **COMMUNICATIVE** CREATURE. A GEMINI IS ALSO AN **INQUISITIVE** ANIMAL. YOU CAN COUNT ON GEMINI CATS BEING THE **MOST** CURIOUS OF ALL THE SIGNS! THEY JUST HAVE TO INVESTIGATE **EVERYTHING!** THIS FELINE MAY GET BORED QUICKLY.

**T**he Gemini cat is ruled by Mercury, god of communication, intelligence, daily activity and media. When it is called, this star cat usually comes running super-quick because a Gemini puss is **always** interested in what's going on. Also, it figures, it's great to have interaction with you (but, as you probably know, not for intense or prolonged periods) because it genuinely likes you.

Your star puss insists that you are to be congratulated on this endeavor to find out more about it, adding that an astro-profile is an excellent way to go about this: "Additional knowledge and understanding can only further improve the quality of our already good lifestyle together—especially, esteemed owner, when you learn more about the quicksilver brilliance of my nature."

This is a **busy** cat, involved in multifarious activities and only stopping now and then for a brief catnap. Gemini kitties are particularly busy when it is sunny and warm. The sun really energizes them, and their interest in things and activity speeds up then. On the other hand, when it is cold, wet and dismal sleep is more interesting to this star cat and it is then capable of sleeping for **extremely** long periods. Your kitty does enjoy sitting in front of a fire with you, too. Sometimes it will stare into the flames, watching the fire as it flicks and burns, sparkles and flares. Your cat urgently wishes to elaborate: "My multifaceted personality is a little like the action of the fire, scintillating and unable to be nailed down, except

I'm more breezy than those belonging to the fire element, like Aries, Leo or Sagittarius cats. They tend to get passionately involved with things and can burn out, whereas I'll just move on to the next thing if a situation isn't working out."

Gemini cats take a keen interest in what's going on around them. In kitten days they not only drove **you** up the wall with their non-stop antics—the kitten in the ball of yarn?: that's a Gemini kitten for sure—but also themselves. Your feline interjects: "It's so difficult not being able to stay still!"

A Gemini cat is super-alert. Nothing gets past this puss' sharp eyes and usually it's attuned to any noise around it, too. You can see your Geminian creature's ears twitching and rotating to home in on incoming sounds. If you watch your pet closely you'll see it responding to audio-stimulation **you** don't hear! This cat constantly monitors its environment. Consequently it's very in touch with what's happening around the place. Your cat whispers to me that you observe this sometimes as you watch it sitting very still, its ears scanning for sound and its eyes rapidly noting any movement. Your kitty moves quickly as well. Quite often it's a case of now you see it, now you don't. The Gemini star cat is fully alive and involved with life.

Your star pet is more devoted to you than you probably think. It's likely that you can communicate more with each other through mutual eye contact than through physical contact. (Sometimes this cat likes to be patted and fussed over, sometimes not. Often it doesn't.) So next time your pet's clear, intelligent eyes are engaged with yours, take a good look and you'll see the regard and love it holds for you. The Gemini puss can enjoy being talked to as well. It likes the sound of your voice and sometimes it'll talk back! This is a highly communicative creature.

A Gemini is also an inquisitive animal. You can count on Gemini cats being the **most** curious of all the signs! They just have to investigate **everything**! This pussycat may get bored quickly, but being an adventuresome and freedom-loving spirit, a Gemini kitty has no lack of confidence and will approach most things without hesitation. However, it must be pointed out that there is a fine balance in the nervous system of Gemini felines, and when badly teased, tormented or confined, their well-being can rapidly deteriorate. They become anxious and nervous, go right off their food, and can become sick. So, however it expresses its unhappiness, please don't let your cat be subject to unfair treatment. Your Gemini feline desires to add something: "And since my usual attitude towards life is happy and optimistic, you miss out on a ray of light (me!) that will brighten and enrich your life, too."

The Gemini cat is normally pretty adaptable, so it usually has no problem living in a house where there are numerous people coming and going and there's lots of activity. In fact, it enjoys it. Whoops! Your pet thinks more should be said: "That is, of course, as long as I'm not negatively stimulated by harassment such as teasing." Catus geminus can also cope well with shifts. (There are actually Gemini cats who live on the road with their RV owners!) But it's best to alert them to an impending change of home beforehand and make sure they are settled afterwards.

The neighborhood fascinates your curious cat. It will often go off on little investigative tours that you may or may not know about. The cat desires the narrative again: "The way you might find out about my exploring is when next door's dog chases me out yet again! (I'm clever, though. I could slip by him if I wanted to. Sometimes I just want the adrenaline rush.) I've been known to peer through windows of nearby houses, and that's simply because I want to see what they are up to. I'm not really nosy or a peeping tom, it's just that movement and activity are the spice of life to me, and I have to keep tabs on **all** that's happening in my world." The Geminian kitty is the type of cat to go for walks with its owner, such is its eagerness for fact-finding missions of any sort.

This star cat can be rather changeable. (Your Gemini cat prefers the term "versatile.") For example, you can feed it something every day for a month, then up goes its nose and it just will **not** eat it. You try again a week later and it's a repeat performance. But offer that same food a few months later and you'll be astounded as Gemini puss tucks into it with appreciative gusto. Your cat urgently wants the narrative: "But that's just me. I always like to keep my options on everything completely flexible. So remember, if you want a witty, cute, charming and entertaining cat who will keep you forever amused, then you've got it with me."

You have a highly inventive animal—just look at the way it's commandeered the narrative!—one that can at times outguess you! But Gemini cat is a friendly and affectionate as well as clever creature. This star cat has a tendency to stay forever fresh in its approach to life and is able to keep you that way, too. The magic of Catus geminus comes in a direct line from Thoth, ancient Egypt's Mercury. Never underestimate it. Just be careful that your special pet's nervous system is not subject to nervous tension. Also, provide high-protein food, vary the diet and ensure your puss has adequate sleep so that all your feline's wonderful abilities unfold.

# CANCER *cat*

22 June–23 July

**herb:** Tarragon

**stone:** Pearl

**number:** 2

**element:** Water—would like to be a temple cat

**celebrity cat:** Disraeli—Florence Nightingale's cat

NATURALLY, WHAT SUSTAINS THIS STAR FELINE IS LOVE AND ACKNOWLEDGMENT. WHEN THE CANCERIAN KITTY GETS ENOUGH NURTURING, IT BLOSSOMS INTO A **VIBRANT**, **HEALTHY** AND **INTRIGUING** ANIMAL. YOUR PUSS IS MUCH BETTER ABLE TO TAP INTO ITS LARGE STORE OF WISDOM WHEN FEELING SAFE AND SECURE. AS ITS SYMPATHETIC OWNER, YOU CAN SENSE IT, AND ALSO SEE A "KNOWING-NESS" IN ITS EYES. **INTUITION** IS A STRONG PART OF CATUS CANCERIA'S NATURE, TOO, AND AGAIN WHEN ITS WORLD FEELS RIGHT THIS FACULTY WORKS A LOT BETTER.

**T**he Cancer cat is ruled by the Moon, goddess of emotion, magnetism and the family principle. When it is called, this cat generally puts in an appearance sooner or later, once the message pierces its active inner world.

Your cat would like to thank you, its beloved owner, for going to so much trouble to find out more about its sensitive, loving, sometimes dreamy nature. Now you will have extra understanding about your puss that will make the feeling between you even better. Your life together will flow with increased smoothness and satisfaction. Your star cat urgently wishes to add: "Plus I **need** to know you love me, and your reading this astro-profile on me shows me you do!" I'll bet you can hear your kitty purring now.

Perhaps at times you find your Cancerian feline hard to fathom. One day it'll be walking tall and strong, and the next it'll look worried and fearful. That's because, like the tides, its confidence is sometimes in, sometimes out. Its moods and feelings change with the Moon. (Your cat interjects: "**You** find it difficult to handle! What about me?") Cancerian kitties are not usually combative because so much of their energy has to focus on sorting out what's going on in their inner world. Unfortunately, this can make it easy for other animals to bully them; people, too. Aggression confuses these cats and makes it harder for them to deal with what they feel, so often they'll respond to harshness by running away.

Naturally, what sustains this star feline is love and acknowledgment. When the Cancerian kitty gets enough nurturing, it blossoms into a vibrant, healthy and intriguing animal. Your puss is much better able to tap into its large store of wisdom when feeling safe and secure. As its sympathetic owner, you can sense it, and also see a "knowingness" in its eyes. Intuition is a strong part of Catus canceria's nature, too, and again when its world feels right this faculty works a lot better. When it isn't being short-circuited by fear and apprehension, your cat's natural ability to feel the future functions easily and it glows with the promise in life. Your star cat can then inspire you with its strength and confidence to handle anything that is going on and also boost your capacity to enjoy life. This puss can be a very special animal, being in tune with the moon as it is.

Oh, gosh! Your cat is pressing to have another say: "Don't misunderstand anything. I derive enormous happiness from life, particularly—as has already been mentioned—when my emotional world is balanced." [Actually, when this is the case, a Cancer puss can become quite bossy!—*Author*.] "I am possessed of a great sense of drama and humor—the cat that sailed off with the owl under the moon was definitely a Cancer creature! I am extremely sensitive to you and have a finely tuned sense of timing, smooching up to you just when you need a bit of love (and at other times, too!), or coming to find you when I sense you're a bit down (I expect the same from you). By the way, I forget neither a kindness nor a hurt. When my confidence is robust I repay both. As well as lots of lovingness I'm capable of vengefulness, as some hapless creatures (like the dog!) find out."

Food is of the utmost importance to Cancer cats. They look forward to their mealtimes, and will remind you vociferously if you are a little tardy on delivery. This puss enjoys milk (and cream) with its food, too. Although not a terribly fussy eater, a Cancer feline does have its culinary standards, and there are some things it will refuse. Your kitty murmurs: "Cat food from the really low end of the market is something I have trouble stomaching." This love of food tends to ensure a physically substantial creature, although some Cancer cats can be reasonably ethereal. Yet, whether big or small, they can give an ethereal impression anyway because their oft-times dreamy, imaginative gaze indicates a focus into other worlds.

Another important factor in your star cat's life (always remember that love is the most important thing of all for it) is sleep. They like lots of it, preferably in comfortable places. Cancer cats enjoy sunshine but will seek moonlight as well. They love the night and will often want to go out in it (particularly if it's not too cold or wet). Your cat adds: "My soul likes to chase shadows in the night."

The home and household is **extremely** close to your kitty's heart. When anything goes awry there it can get worried and fretful. But if it can think of how to help, then it'll try to. Your feline whispers: "Fortunately things are not often amiss, and our home is mostly a place of happiness and plenty." The Cancer cat will frequently go on domestic patrol, checking everything out—into the corners, under the bed, a look in the linen closet, behind the doors. In fact, it will make a thorough inspection! It also likes to sit in the kitchen and watch what you're doing. Food preparation intrigues this star cat, plus kitchen smells are ambrosia to it. Your cat quietly chips in: "Besides, I like to be with you."

Cuddles, affection and closeness are obviously very important to Cancer cats. Their back arches, their tail quivers, their ears bristle, their purr rattles when you're giving them a good pat. They behave the same way when rubbing happily against your legs. These pusses adore being scratched under the chin. And unlike some other cats, most Cancer cats like to be held. They will lie in your arms or rest their paws on your shoulder, blissfully purring while you hold them close and warm, whispering nice things in their ear. If they are allowed, snuggling in bed with you is another favorite.

Cancer kitties are reasonably gentle and patient with children, but they do become crabby if too harassed. Then they are liable to bite as well as scratch. Catus canceria is nostalgic and sentimental about its adopted family and is disinclined to wander far. Identifying strongly with its home and hearth definitely deters them from this. Incidentally, this also means that your cat pours a lot of love and calm energy into what it considers to be "our house."

Altogether, this is a cat that is thoroughly worthy of its place in your affections, and all you give your puss will be repaid with coin in kind. Your pet wants to say: "Thank you again for loving me."

### PAWNOTES:

Your pet is a downright sterling animal. As you have been made well aware, the emotional well-being of this cat is central to its overall health and capability. So do be certain to give your cat unstinted affection, plus reassurance, and you will find yourself with a rather incredible, loving feline companion. Your Cancer kitty can be the source of much strength, related as it is to the star cats that used to wait upon Ishtar, the ancient Babylonian goddess who is regarded as the personification of love and fruitfulness.

# LEO *cat*

24 July–23 August

**herb:** Dandelion

**stone:** Diamond

**number:** 1

**element:** Fire—was born to rule

**celebrity cat:** Miss Puss Puss—Zsa Zsa Gabor's cat

LEO CATS **ADORE** THE SUN. LION-LIKE THEY BASK IN ITS RAYS. CONCRETE WALLS, LARGE ROCKS—IN FACT, ANY PROMINENT OUTCROPPING REACHING TOWARDS THE SUN— ARE FAVORITE POSITIONS OF THIS STAR PUSS. AND YET, WHEN IT GETS TOO HOT THE SHADOW SIDE SUITS THEM JUST AS WELL. "AFTER ALL," SAYS YOUR CAT, "I CONTINUE TO LOOK REGAL WHEREVER I AM." DURING WINTER A LEO PUSS WILL TAKE UP A POSITION IN FRONT OF THE FIRE. PRIDE OF PLACE ON THE SOFA IS ANOTHER FAVORITE SPOT, AND YOUR **WARM**, SNUGGLY LAP IS A PERENNIAL **DELIGHT**.

The Leo cat is ruled by the Sun, god of love, life and vitality. This star cat has an abundance of all three, as you probably well know. Gold belongs to the Sun, too; the metal is seen as representative of distilled sunshine. Your puss figures that should give you further clues to its **royal** lineage. When you call your cat it usually doesn't take too long in strolling up because it knows something good is bound to be in store.

Your cat confides in me that it's great that you are creative enough to think of going through its astro-profile. (Then it whispers: "Not that I ever doubted they were special anyway. I've got excellent taste!") By reading this, you can learn even more about what a terrific cat you call your own, although sometimes it can be questionable who owns whom! Also your pet now has the opportunity to inform you of things about them that you might not realize. Like for example, your feline reckons that it deserves the best because it **is** the best. (In an aside to me your puss says for you to "disregard what Aries cats say on this matter.") And offers another example: "Do you know that I can make a great circus cat if I have to? And even so, I certainly know a trick or two!"

Leo cats **adore** the sun. Lion-like they bask in its rays. Concrete walls, large rocks—in fact, any prominent outcropping reaching towards the sun—are favorite positions of this star puss. And yet, when it gets too hot the shadow side suits them just as well. "After all," says your cat, "I continue to look regal wherever I am." During winter a Leo puss will take up a position in front of the fire. Pride of place on the sofa is another favorite spot, and your warm, snuggly lap is a perennial delight. And your cat wants it said that, fine-looking animal that it is, it graces any place or situation with its presence.

This star cat does like to be appreciated. (Leo cats will do quite a lot for attention. That's part of the reason they make good performers.) The more members there are in their fan club the better. Your cat interjects: "After all, I am a star." True. And that can usually be seen in its fine form, proud style and dramatic ways. (The Persian in the cat food advertisement is a Leo, you bet!) But do remember that your feline has a great heart and will radiate love back to you. In fact, it can inspire you with its strongly evident powerful and fiery love. Your kitty's feeling for you is a constant, even though it may not always seem that way to you. At such times it is probably momentarily pouting over some obtuse slight to Catus leonus' romantic, amorous and sometimes vain nature.

Leo kitties tend to form likes or dislikes on first contact. Once they have made their mind up about a person, another animal, situation or whatever, then that's it! They are **for** it or them to the death or **against** it or them with total anathema. It takes a miracle to change the Leo puss' attitude.

When they do "like," then they can be a little demanding. Some Leo cats can actually be rather brash as they walk into a room, loudly commanding attention. They get it, too! People do respond to a confident, self-assured, positive creature that knows what it wants. Other Leo cats are more alert to the politics in any situation and work through these dynamics. Therefore they can actually be more powerful in attaining their ends. But there's definitely a magnanimous streak to the Leonine pussy's nature. Your cat chimes in: "And this can be observed—whenever any person has anything to do with me, they are left feeling better from the contact. Also my ways bring smiles to many faces, and I am often the cause of happy laughter."

This is a strong, brave animal (although there is the odd Leo that is a "scaredy cat"—a bit like the lion in the *Wizard of Oz*, all bluster and no follow-through). This star cat likes to exercise its limbs; it will even frolic around the garden at times, particularly at sunset. But it also revels in the chance to sleep. Your puss will lie somewhere and refresh its energies with a siesta. (Hang on. Your cat's exploding to say something: "What's all this 'lazy lump' stuff! That's not me you're thinking of. Is it?") Leo kitties will visit their many kingdoms in the astral realms, which can sometimes take a while, then return to their castle (it doesn't matter what you live in, to your cat, it's a "castle") on the earthly plane. Ready for cuddles, happiness, good feelings and a little snack.

Your puss would like to have a say: "I enjoy my food. I'm quite a sensuous, not to mention beautiful, beast actually. I have a great lust for life and take pleasure on many levels of existence." This star cat is not usually a picky eater, but like many cats it prefers quality food. The Leo feline likes its liquids, too.

Leos are not normally wanderers. Their home and household are too central in importance for that. Leo puss is reasonably territory-minded and can get quite aggressive with those who breach its domain. But at heart this is not a mean-minded or malicious animal. The Leo star cat has a sunny and generous nature and, when it gives its trust, it does so completely. Your cat has more to say: "You can see this in my eyes. My frank, candid gaze at you says it all. We have chosen to be together in our cat and person partnership. You are my special person, and I am your special pet. I recognize things about you that others may not see. I love you forever."

Children can have a lot of fun and delight with this pussikins, and your cat likes them in return. But when Leo felines don't want to be bothered by small people, it's best to leave them alone. Leo cats can get very grumpy and grouchy.

Your cat is pleased that now you can understand (and "appreciate") it a bit better, that you have more insight into its warm and ardent nature and realize that your cat is a positive addition to life.

PAWNOTES:

Well, there you have it. Your fabulous feline has done a great promotional job in helping me give you the big picture on the Leo cat personality. The fact that it sat beside the Pharaoh, as the incarnation of Ra, the ancient Egyptian sun god, probably still resonates on some level. However, the bottom line hasn't quite been spelt out. And that is, your pet is most anxious to be liked by you. So believe it or not, this apparently assured (sometimes to the point of arrogance!) cat actually needs your love and reassurance. Your love will be magically returned to you, many times magnified. But take care not to feed your wonderful animal too many rich and fatty foods because the heart can become a danger zone.

# VIRGO *cat*

24 August–23 September

**herb:** Fennel

**stone:** Lapis lazuli

**number:** 11

**element:** Earth—wants to find out "who threw pussy in the well"

**celebrity cat:** Simkins—Beatrix Potter's puss, always busy with housekeeping and keeping everything tidy

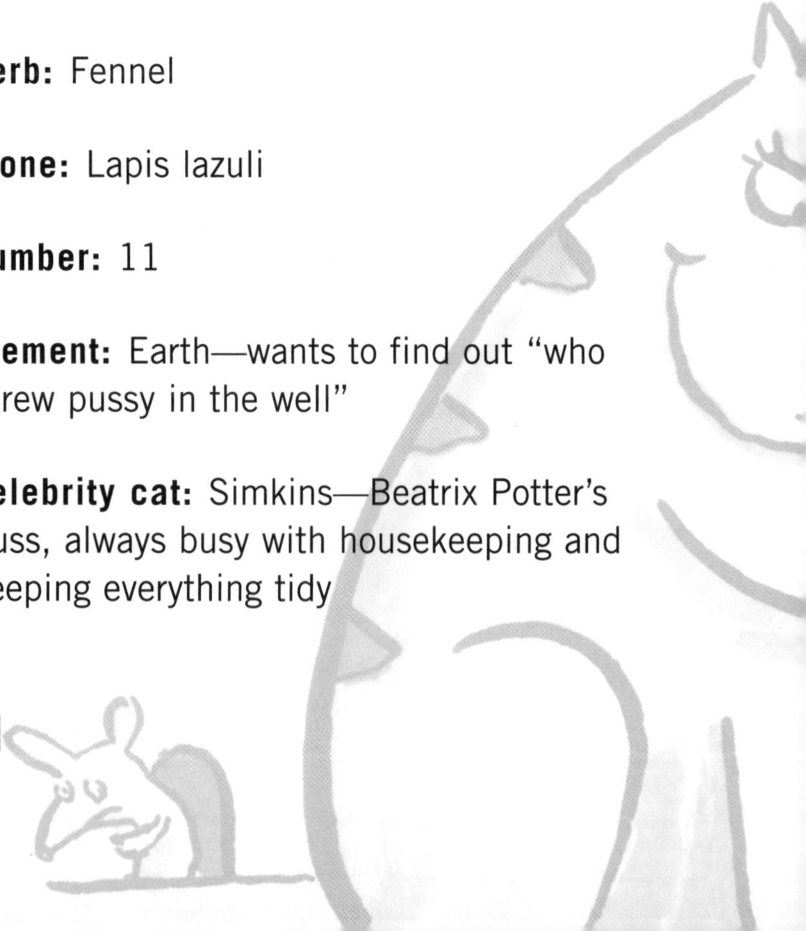

BECAUSE OF YOUR CAT'S CRITICAL QUALITIES, WHICH ARE LINKED TO ITS DRIVE FOR **PERFECTION**, IF YOUR STAR PUSS CAUSES YOU DISPLEASURE OR ANNOYANCE AND IS THEREFORE GROWLED AT, THEN IT CAN FRET SO MUCH THAT IT LOSES ALL CONDITION AND BECOMES **NERVOUS** AND TWITCHY. IT'S A GREAT DEAL MORE PRODUCTIVE TO SHOW YOUR PET WHAT IT IS DOING WRONG AND WHAT IT SHOULD BE DOING. ALSO IF YOU TALK TO YOUR VIRGOAN FELINE CALMLY AND STEADILY, THAT HELPS TREMENDOUSLY. THIS ZODIAC STAR TRIBE ANIMAL HAS A GREAT DEAL OF INNATE **WISDOM**.

**T**he Virgo cat is ruled by Mercury, god of intelligence, deductive analysis, detail and communication. Mercury rules Gemini also but Mercury's slightly more serious earth side governs Virgo, as does its healing and service. When your star cat hears you call, it normally runs up at once, as it's a signal that you have something to see to together. And, it must be said, they view it as a chance to be with you as well.

Your star puss wants me to communicate how happy it is that you care enough to want to find out more about your pet's sometimes puzzling nature. The Virgo cat is more complex than it appears at first sight. And, the way they see it, your understanding and further perception of it will enable it to be a better pet and companion, plus help your cat–person relationship become even more ideal.

The Virgoan feline may seem undemonstrative at times. It can appear less ebullient or outgoing in its affections than other cats. When this is the case please don't let its behavior deceive you. It would be difficult to find a more dedicated and devoted cat than this star creature. What is likely to be going on in the aforementioned instance is that they are internally preoccupied (sometimes referred to as "worried") with the detail of its life, your life and your life together. Your cat wants to explain: "For example, I may move away from your outstretched hand because my last wash was an hour ago and I don't feel clean enough. Or it may be that I'm so concerned about last night's new brand of food not being up to par that I am anxious about tonight's coming meal and I have no feelings left over for loving contact. This is simply my nature. There's not a lot I can do about it. But **you** can, just by understanding my ways and appreciating me for what I am. I am normally a modest creature, but I must say to you that a Virgo cat was much prized in ancient times for the purity of spirit and devotion paid to its owner. In other words, I am the sort of cat who will stay with you through thick and thin."

Well, that's pretty clear. Now I can continue. Because of your cat's critical qualities, which are linked to its drive for perfection, if your star puss causes you displeasure or annoyance and is therefore growled at, then it can fret so much that it loses all condition and becomes nervous and twitchy. It's a great deal more productive to show your pet what it's doing wrong and what it should be doing. Also if you talk to your Virgoan feline calmly and steadily, that helps tremendously.

This Zodiac star tribe animal has a great deal of innate wisdom (the cat that accompanied Merlin was a Virgo cat). When its daily life is sufficiently calm and its nervous system is not stressed out and tense, then this wisdom can flow. You feel it and see instances of it. Your cat's steady eyes hold many answers. Your pet wishes to take up the pen again: "By the way, I'm also an animal connected to a healing vibration—Hippocrates made sure he had a Virgo cat, you know. When all is well in my world I am a transmitter of healing and curing energy."

The Virgo cat is usually a most neat and tidy animal, both in hygiene and appearance. A considerable quantity of time is spent grooming. Every part of your puss is paid a lot of attention. There are no quick licks for this cat. The ears almost glisten; its claws gleam; every part of it is spic and span.

Food-wise your star pet can be a little exasperating until you find what combination works for it. Your puss doesn't mean to be fussy and finicky, it's just that its tummy isn't happy with any old food. Its nourishment must have a clean and pure basis. Sometimes a quality cat food with a cereal component will suit the Virgoan digestive system beautifully. They like the right amount of milk; actually some Virgoan felines really enjoy yogurt. Often a feeding schedule of frequent small servings suits this cat better than one or two big meals a day.

Being a cat with definite investigative leanings, the Virgoan feline's little nose usually gets into everything that is new or curious (not strange people, though—this star puss tends to be initially shy and cautious). Catus virgous always likes to find out **what** and **why**! Your puss eagerly wants to elaborate: "Agatha Christie was not a member of Catus domesticus, but she was a **Virgo**! That tells you something about my grey cells!" The Virgoan kitty can be hyperenergetic in its pursuit of the facts of a situation. It is certainly **mobile** when on the track of something intriguing. But, chances are, you find your pet's inquiring personality rather refreshing. At times it amuses you greatly. This cat can also be rather persuasive when trying to convince you they simply **have** to check something out, and you should let them.

A Virgoan is usually a gentle and well-behaved creature. Your kitty murmurs to me: "I'm not **too** rowdy, noisy or otherwise disgusting!" It's usually polite with little ones and can be very loving. However, the delicate nervous systems of these animals can become horribly jangled from too much noise or teasing. Not that they then become bad scratchers, but their health and unique abilities will suffer. Your cat is really pushing for a say now: "And I have only special gifts to bring you, my revered and beloved owner. In whatever way possible, I will help you. Likely you are unaware of the many ways in which I do add my power to your causes. I seek to be of eternal service to you. To understand what I mean, think of the classic example of the country cat that always deposits its prey outside the kitchen backdoor. The Virgo cat, yes definitely Virgo, does this in service of its master—not that I am one who lives to hunt. That's the job of an Aries feline."

A further priceless gift is the love your Virgo kitty bears for you. And this from a cat that is certainly not indiscriminate in affection—on the contrary, it can sometimes be extraordinarily selective about who it associates with. Towards those it likes, a Virgo pussikins can be very affectionate and caring. This is as much in the quality of feeling as in physical interaction. Your feline wishes to add: "For you, my esteemed and cherished owner, the love I hold is unwavering. The dedicated force of it will be with you as long as I live."

A Virgo cat has oodles of character, and your pet certainly hasn't missed its quota! This unassuming animal has chipped in with modest clarification of its special qualities. This charmingly civil modesty probably derives from its association with Ptah, the ancient Egyptian god who attended the processes of creation, and who was known as Vulcan, god of the arts of forging and smelting in the Roman pantheon. Unquestionably, a loving Virgo feline is a dear and precious creature, one whose heart beats in time with the universe and in love of you. And one who can work special wizardry when you really need it. But, as already mentioned, do watch food quality and intake, because the digestive system tends to be delicate, especially if the cat is unsettled.

# LIBRA *cat*

24 September–23 October

**herb:** Pennyroyal

**stone:** Opal

**number:** 3

**element:** Air—can often be a celebrity cat

**celebrity cat:** Chanoine—Victor Hugo's cat (who sat on a red ottoman and received guests at Parisian winter literary gatherings)

RELATIONSHIPS AND ATTENTION ARE **MOST** IMPORTANT TO LIBRAN KITTIES. THEY CAN BECOME QUITE MELANCHOLY IF YOU DON'T GIVE THEM LOVE, ATTENTION AND AFFECTION. BUT WATCH YOUR STAR CAT GO WHEN YOU DO! THEN YOUR PET PURRS WITH POISE, **CONFIDENCE** AND **RADIANCE**. YOUR CAT IS BURSTING TO SAY SOMETHING: "I'M ALWAYS AT MY BEST WHEN I'M ADMIRED. THAT'S WHY A LOT OF US LIBRANS ARE **TERRIFIC** SHOW CATS. WE WIN, TOO." THE BEAUTIFUL, LUXURIOUS-LOOKING FELINE IN **ANY** TOP-NOTCH AD IS A LIBRAN CAT FOR CERTAIN.

**T**he Libran cat is ruled by Venus, goddess of peace, harmony, beauty and love. When you call your cat, it will usually saunter up because it knows that this normally signals that something good is about to happen.

It is tremendously nice of you, your star cat would like it made known, that you're making this effort to find out more about it. On the other hand, it figures that since it is such a fascinating, sophisticated creature, how could you do otherwise than take advantage of this opportunity to further illumine their fabulous personality? Actually, if you hadn't, your Libran pussikins would have been hurt. Your pet wants to explain: "That would have indicated you didn't love me enough, and that the **great** love I hold for you was misplaced." Fortunately, that is obviously **not** the case, and any tiny insecurities are now quelled. Your cat eagerly interrupts: "So, let's go on to talk more about me. The better you know me, the better our relationship will be."

I suppose it's best to say right off that Librans can be paradoxical creatures. Your puss adds: "I mean, peace is so important to me that I'll go to war for it!" Love is the center of this star cat's universe, and yet sometimes it may seem cool and uninterested in you. Perhaps it will be rowdy and robust one time, then sensitive and withdrawn the next. Enthusiasm can be this feline's middle name, then another time in the same situation it can be quite detached. The list could go on and on, but you get the drift. ("You don't have to say 'And how!' " your cat interjects.) Keep in mind that the Balances, or Scales, if you prefer, are associated with this sign, and you may begin to get some insight on this. Catus librus is always weighing things up and can get lost in the process. Sometimes it overbalances to one extreme or the other, and subsequent behavior can be confusing to those concerned. "But overall," your puss elaborates, "I usually balance everything harmoniously, and create a good effect for us all."

The next important thing to point out is that relationships and attention are **most** important to Libran felines. They can become quite melancholy if you don't give them love, attention and affection. But watch your star cat go when you do! Then your pet purrs with poise, confidence and radiance. Your cat is bursting to say something: "I'm always at my best when I'm admired. That's why a lot of us Librans are terrific show cats. We win, too. The beautiful, luxurious-looking feline in **any** top-notch ad is a Libran cat for certain. We can be simply glorious, and we know it, too. The composure and cool of a Libran cat has sold many a product, inspired poetry, and brought many a human to their knees." Well said! Your pet is not exaggerating.

Libran kitties need to be petted and loved (even if they don't seem to particularly lap it up, most times they do) and will sensuously invite your attentions by twining their warm and furry bodies around your legs. Sleep and relaxation are important in these cats' lives, too—preferably on feather down, velvet cushions and silk sheets. Sleep helps keep Libra felines' eyes lustrous and their coats glossy, and it takes them closer to their dreams. Your star cat wants to communicate: "I always wake delightfully energized from my slumber, bringing more calm, happiness and beauty to our relationship and household."

Generally speaking, cats of the Libran star tribe are quite popular. People remark on what beauties they are. Catus librus does not have to be a purebred to convey a pedigree impression. Often it will have a special relationship with certain friends of yours. It's not that your Libran creature loves you any less, only that it thrives on interaction with people it likes. This star cat is mostly polite with visitors, but there is the odd person (or animal) they will take a dislike to. The **disdain** of a Libran puss can be quite palpable. ("Did you really have to say 'snooty?'" your cat murmurs. I think it's addressing you, not me.) But being a sociable beast it tends to sparkle in the company of guests, and the visitors definitely enjoy your cat. When your cat decides it's had enough, it will just stroll away.

Your feline's appetites for life and experience include the food department. The Libran cat is not normally a finicky eater, but it does prefer quality. You can count on this pussy cat opting for the most expensive food and the best. (Your cat's interjecting again: "Top-notch **everything** is my choice. See a cat in a diamond collar and that's sure to be a Libra creature.") The same as any other puss, it looks forward to its milk and cream. However, it can also be one of those cats that **love** ice cream. If it's Haagen-Dazs ice cream, no less, we can bet the cat is a Libran. Some Libran kitties have been known to nibble chocolate! "Try me sometime," says your cheeky cat.

With children the Libran kitty is usually fine. It isn't a nasty cat and can be reasonably compliant with kids' activities. "As long as," Libran puss adds, "they don't become too absurd." Then it spiritedly continues: "But the one thing I cannot **stand** is to have my fur rubbed the wrong way. The cat with arched back and eyes ablaze is me if that happens. I'm quite a strong creature—despite how deceptively cute and lovely I may look—so don't let me get to that state. Someone could get hurt."

The home and household matter to your pussikins. And it is probably more sensitive to what's going on than you realize. Any discordant vibrations can upset this cat greatly. (Your pet wants to elaborate further: "I'm quite subtle in my awareness about most things, so not everything that I, as your cat, know and feel may be obvious. But if you genuinely seek to find out what I know, I can be reached.") Particularly disturbances of a loud or ugly nature. Gosh. Your cat's after the narrative again! "Don't worry. Our house is normally a place that has a special dimension of beauty to it (that too may not be obvious), and you can trust me to find and highlight that beauty. I also frequently channel beautiful, peaceful and harmonious vibrations into our living space." So you can see, dear owner, that underneath all appearances to the contrary, your star pet loves you devotedly, and also likes to focus on enhancing the beauty of togetherness with you.

The Libran cat is an attractive animal, one with considerable charm and grace. This is a feline possessed of an ability to somehow sweeten life, and they have chosen to join forces with you. Your pet wants to finish with these words: "Let's enjoy life together, and I'll show you what I can do."

No doubt about it. You have a winner here. But to
cultivate a harmonious relationship with your Libra cat,
you have to meet your pet's requirements, which have
been set out fairly explicitly. Otherwise this cat might just
look elsewhere. Your loss would definitely be someone
else's gain since this puss, as well as being a loving and
charming companion, brings love to life. This probably
comes from its attendance at the court of Isis, the
powerful goddess whose loving relationship with Osiris was
pivotal to ancient Egyptian cosmological understanding.
But do make sure that your cat is given only clean and
pure liquids because the kidneys can be a sensitive area.

# SCORPIO *cat*

24 October–22 November

9½ lives

**herb:** Basil

**stone:** Topaz

**number:** 10

**element:** Water—has deep knowledge of the occult

**celebrity cat:** Catarina—Edgar Allen Poe's cat

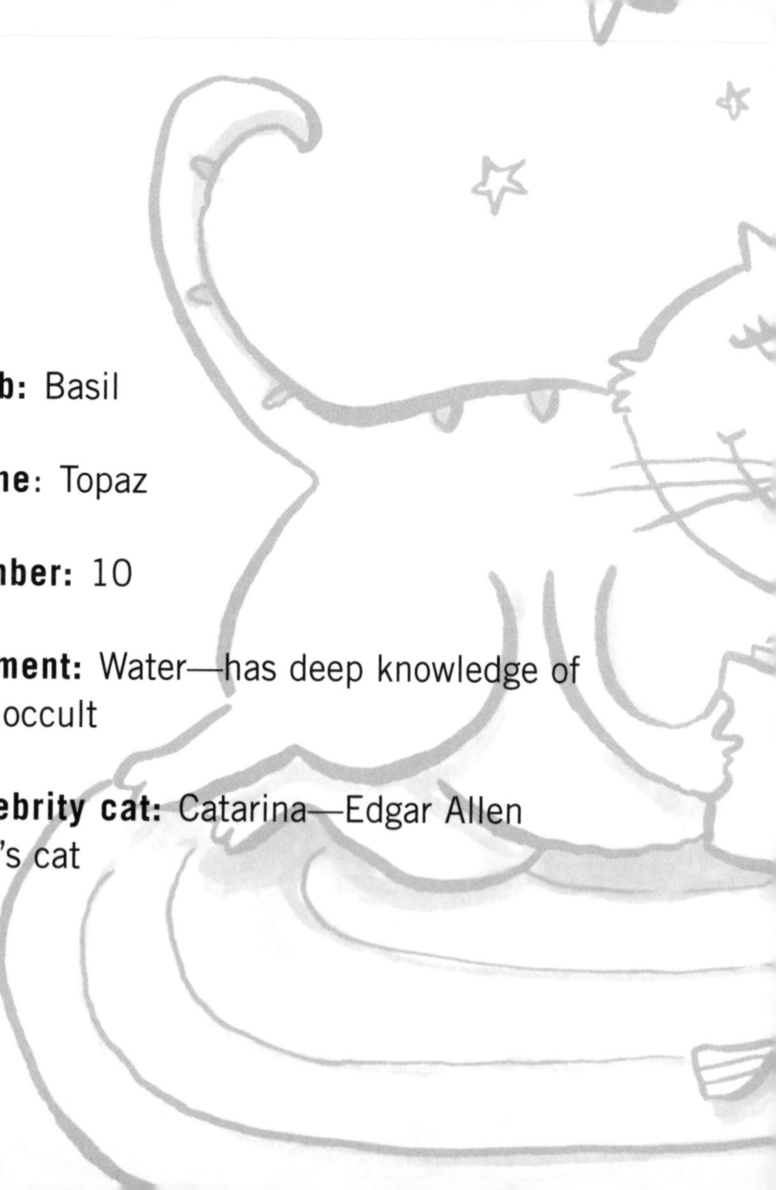

CATUS SCORPIUS' FOCUS TOWARDS LIFE IS **INTENSE**. THIS CAN BE A STRANGE ANIMAL. AT TIMES IT CAN SEEM AS REMOTE AND VEILED AS DEATH ITSELF. A SCORPIO FELINE CARRIES AN AURA OF POWER THAT OTHER ANIMALS (AND SOME PEOPLE) **RESPECT** AND OFTEN **FEAR**. THEY DON'T MESS WITH THIS STAR FELINE BUT INSTEAD TAKE TO THEIR HEELS WHEN THEY SENSE ITS IMMINENT APPROACH. THIS IS NOT REALLY A CAT THAT FIGHTS ON THE PHYSICAL PLANE, ALTHOUGH IT CAN, RUTHLESSLY. THESE ZODIAC STAR TRIBE MEMBERS WIN MOST OF THEIR BATTLES ON THE PSYCHIC PLANE.

he Scorpio cat is ruled by Pluto, god of the mysteries of life, magic and atomic power. When you call your cat, it usually appears soon after because it knows something intensely interesting is about to take place.

Your puss is pleased that you find it sufficiently fascinating to want to seek further understanding of its complex character. Your star cat's feelings for you run very deep, and the more insight you gain into its qualities, the more your destiny together will improve. It knows you well and, happily, now you will know and better appreciate your Scorpio cat.

Catus scorpius' focus towards life is **intense.** This can be a strange animal. At times it can seem as remote and veiled as death itself. A Scorpio feline carries an aura of power that other animals (and some people) respect and often fear. They don't mess with this star feline but instead take to their heels when they sense its imminent approach. This is not really a cat that fights on the physical plane, although it can, ruthlessly. These zodiac star tribe members win most of their battles on the psychic plane. Their secrecy is related to this. Scorpio pusses don't like anyone to know what they are thinking, doing or feeling if they don't want them to. Their eyes reveal nothing when they close the doors behind them.

As for the profound nature of your cat's love for you, your pet has something to reveal: "I am **your** cat, and will provide everything a cat should for its special human, and more. The hidden, untapped aspects to me are quite immense." Your feline's feeling for you is a powerful force that makes it even more directed and capable a creature. But it can tend to be a little possessive. Your cat's tactics with any competition for your affections are not to love you to submission, as would a Taurus cat, but to destroy the opposition, often in ways unseen. Your puss is extremely loyal to you, and would go through hell for you, if that were necessary.

So far all this may give the impression that Catus scorpius has no sense of humor. That's not true. Its approach to the funny side of life is as lusty and passionate as everything else about it. This animal can gain great amusement from watching lesser beings battle against the odds. (But they can be compassionate, too.) Struggles between life and death fascinate this puss, as do all processes of nature. They can enjoy a walk around the grounds with you inspecting the growth in the garden. Sometimes they'll chase after will-o'-the-wisps you can't see. Your cat also likes to observe the behavior of humans. (Not all the time. They like to be alone a lot, too.) Solemnly they will quietly watch what's going on, adding what's noted to their general understanding of humanity. (Scorpio cats have good psychological perception. Sigmund Freud's cat had to have been a Scorpio.) Yet the Scorpio creature can also break out into little frenzies. It can rush out and amaze everybody by spinning around the room in an attempt to be entertaining, or by attacking a guest's shoe or cell phone. Your kitty may not do this often. But **whatever** it does, it is almost invariably incomprehensible or inscrutable.

Scorpio kitties are fairly territorially minded. They don't take kindly to anything impinging on their borders. Being dictatorial concerning what it regards as its own, your puss deals quickly and efficiently with any intruders or challenges. It behaves the same way with food. Heaven help any other cat that dares to approach your feline's bowl while it is feeding. Catus scorpius can have a most malevolent growl. It doesn't forget anything, either. Your cat will wait for the right moment to repay kindness with kindness, and evil actions with revenge. It looks out for your interests here, too.

The Scorpio feline can be an animal possessed of a certain charisma, one that hypnotizes (Mata Hari was not a cat, but she had Scorpio rising) and is attractive to others. At the same time, suspecting all situations to have inherent problems causes this cat to use caution and check everything out, and it can take a while to build trust. This is linked to the fact that Scorpios often have an unusual destiny (Prince Charles belongs to Scorpio, and your cat bets his cat does, too!) so they have to be careful about what they involve themselves with. (Fate is often seen to intervene in the lives of Scorpio felines.) This is a strong, brave and valiant cat that thrives on the challenge of a meaningful life. Your cat desires to add: "Also there is good purpose in our being together. I am not your cat for nothing."

In some ways this cat is a loner. To go its own way and be solitary is occasionally necessary for it. But don't ever worry, your puss will return. (If it doesn't, you will always know why.) Being adventurous, this star cat needs to go off and dabble with fortune now and then. Your pussikins likes to slip out into the night as well. Its chatoyant eyes gleam in the dark and its psychic abilities hone up as it travels around.

Sleep is important to your cat, of course. Your cat wishes to elaborate: "Still, I'm not as enthralled by it as some other cats. Pisces, for example. That critter likes nothing better than to live in dreams!" Food is also an essential part of life, but unlike Virgoan or Geminian cats, Scorpio puss usually takes what it gets with minimal fuss. The home and household is an important focus for your pet. And it does what it can to ensure the heart of the home beats strongly. Your cat's work here can be most effective; nevertheless, you probably know little about it. ("Neither do you have to," your kitty murmurs.)

With small people this puss is usually alright. The cat can find them interesting, too. If they perchance begin to annoy Scorpio puss, it will simply switch off and go away.

So there you have it! Your Scorpio cat. A practical yet mystical and powerful cat. One who feels deeply, and loves you more completely than you perhaps realize. Your cat wants a final word: "I'm with you through rain or shine."

### PAWNOTES:

The Scorpio cat is a tremendously capable and resourceful creature. It is definitely the case that still waters run deep here. No doubt this arises because Scorpio cat occupied a place in the halls of Osiris, the ancient Egyptian god known as king of eternity, ruler of everlastingness. You have a stalwart and at times astonishing animal. Please do take special care to give love and affection, even if the cat doesn't seem to ask for it. You can be sure it is required and will strengthen the unfolding of the life you and your cat have together. Just a word of caution. If you have your pet desexed, be certain to follow your vet's instructions because the procreative organs in Scorpio felines can be problem zones.

# SAGITTARIUS
*cat*

23 November–22 December

**herb:** Sage

**stone:** Turquoise

**number:** 7

**element:** Fire—has terrible timing, but great luck!

**celebrity cat:** Rhubarb—owner died and left him a baseball team

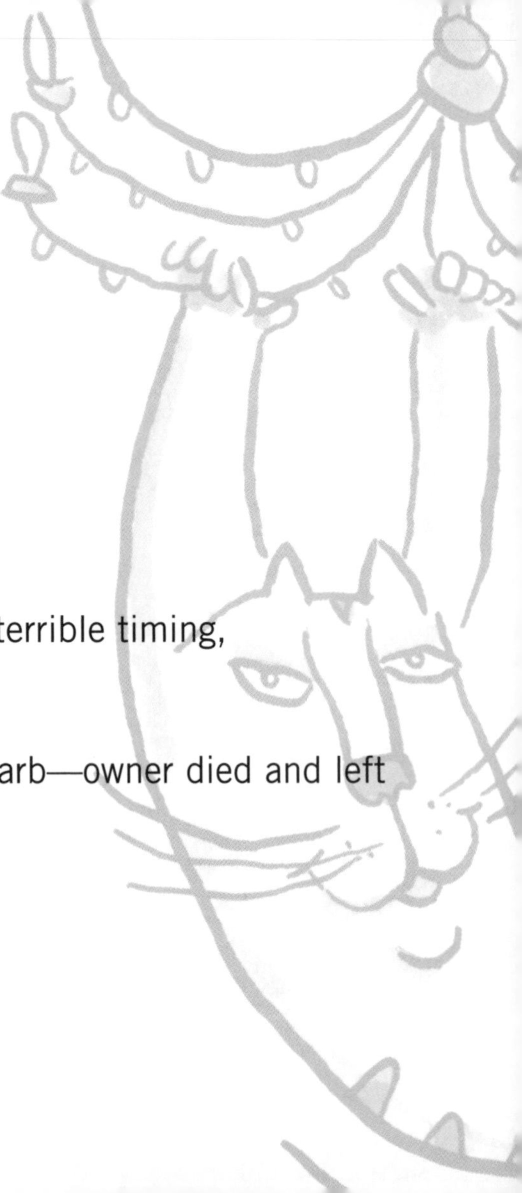

THIS IS A **LOVING**, **GIVING** CAT, BUT NOT ONE THAT IS **SLAVISHLY DEVOTED**. WHEN YOUR ATTENTION IS TAKEN UP BY SOMETHING ELSE, THAT'S OK BY YOUR FELINE. LIFE IS PERENNIALLY CHOCK-FULL OF OPPORTUNITIES FOR A SAGITTARIUS PUSS ANYWAY. AND IT FREQUENTLY PREFERS TO TRAVEL AROUND BY ITSELF, FINDING THERE'S ALWAYS A LOT TO **EXPERIENCE** AND **EXPLORE** IN THE GARDEN, THE HOUSE, OTHER PEOPLE'S HOUSES, OTHER PEOPLE'S GARDENS. IF THERE IS A PARK OR WILD PLACE NEARBY WE CAN BE SURE THAT THIS IS ONE OF ITS HAUNTS AS WELL.

The Sagittarius cat is ruled by Jupiter, god of good fortune, philosophy, joviality and good times. When you call your cat it will normally roll right up (if it's not off voyaging somewhere or involved in an absorbing diversion) because it reckons you could be in for some sort of merriment together. Whatever! Your pet also figures that it's "always great to see you."

Heavens! Your puss has the narrative and is running off with it! "How terrific that you are reading this astro-profile on me! I'm an independent, enchanting and inspirational animal, and it's worthwhile to know more about me so as to derive even more fun and happiness from our association. It will definitely add to our enjoyment together, also make **even** better our situation as cat and person."

Well, now that I've wrested back the narrative, let me say the Sagittarius cat is usually an optimistic, positive creature, and one that's almost constantly in motion—always busy going somewhere. Puss'n' boots is a good example of a Sagittarius cat. Your pet has the narrative again! "I'm pretty high-spirited, too. (Oh, no! Don't bring up my kitten days. I was simply an ebullient, energized, exuberant creature new to life. I didn't mean to wreck the furniture, rip the curtains, destroy a pot plant or two. But didn't I look **great** hanging off the chandelier! And wasn't it all worth it? You wouldn't swap me for any other cat in the whole world now!) I can lift your spirits as well." Well, your cat is probably correct on all counts. This star cat's eager, joyous approach to life is inspiring and undoubtedly puts a chuckle into many a day for you.

The Sagittarian star cat has a high degree of intuition. When it comes to the bottom line, our puss can be relied on to know how you are—even if it isn't with you. If things are bad for you, chances are your Sagittarian feline will turn up to console or cheer you. (Your pet whispers: "I much prefer the latter," and adds: "Consoling can be left to Pisces and Cancer cats.") It's always this star cat's irrepressible, optimistic nature that comes to the fore (your cat chips in with an afterthought: "Actually I get impatient with **too** much sorrow; life is too precious to wallow in that!"), and it wants you to experience this feeling, too.

To this end Catus sagittarius may engage in some off-the-wall, exhibitionist theater to raise a laugh out of you. Or it will do something else a little different to break your mood. Your cat's got the pen again! "When I'm in super-good shape I can actually guide good luck your way. Fortunately your life doesn't often go badly, but I do these things for you as a matter of course."

This is a loving, giving cat, but not one that is slavishly devoted. When your attention is taken up by something else, that's OK by your feline. Life is perennially chock-full of opportunities for a Sagittarius puss anyway. And it frequently prefers to travel around by itself, finding there's always a lot to experience and explore in the garden, the house, other people's houses, other people's gardens. If there is a park or wild place nearby we can be sure that this is one of its haunts as well. Your cat has eagerly seized the narrative yet again! "I like to sing with the other cats at night, too. It's not fighting I get into (although I can certainly give as good as I get), it's the carousing. (Top Cat was a Sagittarius cat, you know.) All in all, I'm a good-time feline."

Well, your pet **is** looking pleased with itself, and now I can continue. Being an adaptable and fairly outgoing creature, this cat normally doesn't mind meeting new people, within reason. Catus sagittarius can enjoy interaction with other animals, too. There is a lot to life that your pet finds entertaining. Now your kitty's muscling in again: "And I'm pretty popular. Everybody likes me—even the dog! Just my presence can start a happy feeling in people, and even without my **doing** anything people will often say to you, 'That cat of yours is a card.' (Yes, the joker—top trumps.) Perhaps you'd better keep an eye on me because I'm the sort of cat people want to steal away. Really, my karma must be good (well, for starters I'm with you!) because it's so easy for me to have a great time in life and share that with others."

With their range of versatile behavioral options Sagittarian felines are capable of many things deemed unusual in a cat. What now? Alright. The cat figures it can explain this best: "For example,

I absolutely love listening to your music—jazz, opera, rock, country, religious, classical, anything! Just so long as it has some truth content that moves my inner spiritual vision. I'd make a great university cat, too, because I like to listen in on the intelligent discussions you have with your friends. I can give you answers if you'll let me. Sitting beside the fire together in companionable silence is another enjoyable activity. I even enjoy basking in the sun with you. Also, I am the sort of cat capable of going for walks with its owner." To be frank, it's probably best to treat your star pussikins like a lively companion, otherwise it just might stray elsewhere looking for mutual inspiration.

Children and the Sagittarius puss usually get along well, as long as not too much silliness grates on your star cat's nerves. "And I'm positively patriotic about our home and household," your pet enthusiastically chimes in. "True blue as far as I'm concerned." In fact, a Sagittarius cat is the type of cat that can feel so much a part of its family that it will go overseas with them if that's what a house move means. (Sagittarian cats are travelers in more ways than one.) Normally a change of domestic base does not disturb this cat overly much, as a Sagittarian cat is more interested in what goes on in a house, rather than the physical location. (They are capable of making themselves at home anywhere.)

Most Sagittarian felines aren't all that demanding in their food preferences. Having said that, if they happen to develop a liking for something a little different, you may discover they have peculiar taste, like the one who loved Irish coffee, and another who enjoyed sandwiches! They do like their food to appear at reasonably regular times and accompanied by a drink. Sleep, naturally, is important. The normal pattern is that when Sagittarius puss is asleep, it's quite gone, busy hunting in astral realms, and when awake, it's 100 percent up and active. There are always variations on the theme, of course.

Your puss is now politely asking for a say: "But that's life itself, is it not?—variations on a theme." [Wonder if Bach had a Sag. cat?— *Author.*] "Developing the fullness of life together is what we are about. Without any false modesty I can say that I am a charming, happy and lucky cat. One with a lot of spirit, and I have more than enough of what it takes to help you create our special duet in life."

Well, your pet hasn't been unduly extravagant in summing up the qualities it possesses. Except perhaps for giving the impression that all one needs to win the lottery is a Sagittarius cat (although it has been known to happen)! But your puss has pointed out that good luck is related to good karma. And these star cats can seem to have accumulated it in abundance through attending the court of Bes, the Egyptian god with shaggy hair and a tail, often clad in a lion skin, who was the patron of music, jollity, and timely and successful ventures. Bes was extremely popular among the ancient Egyptians. And good karma is definitely what you and your cat can create together.

# CAPRICORN
*cat*

SPY Thriller

DICTIONARY

War and Peace

23 December–20 January

**herb:** Solomon's seal

**stone**: Garnet

**number:** 8

**element:** Earth—always a winner in the long run

**celebrity cat:** Wilderforce—No. 10 Downing Street cat. Served under four British prime ministers

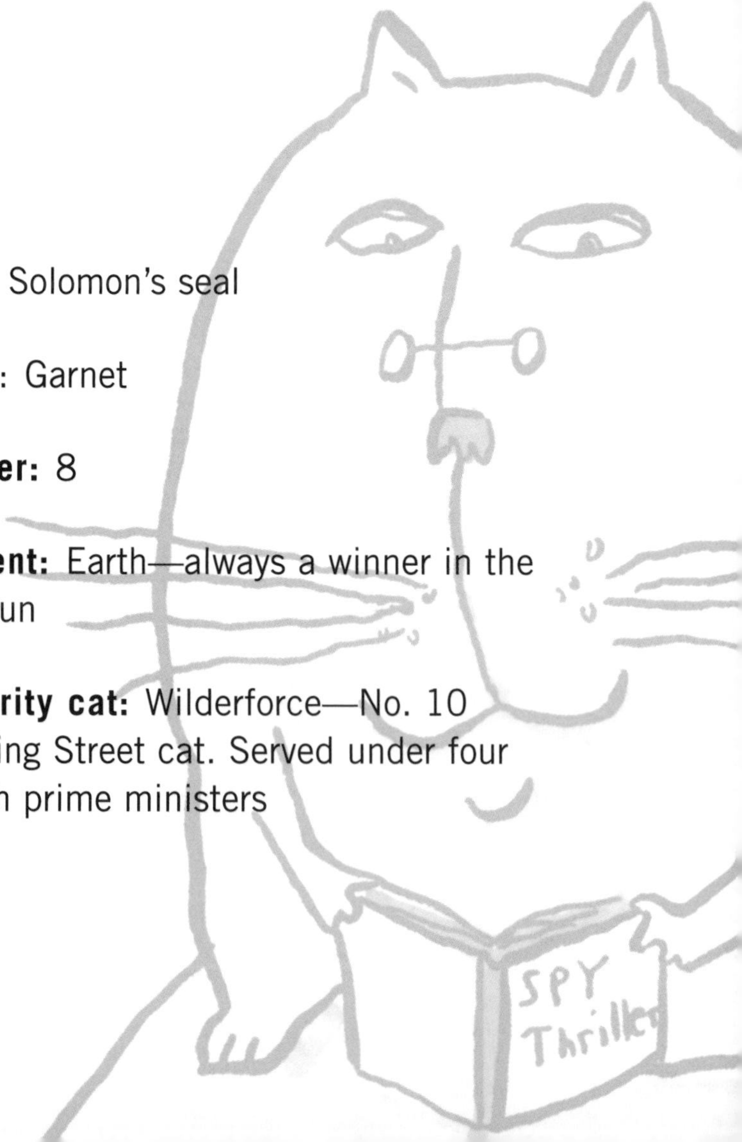

THIS STAR CAT HAS A LARGE APPETITE FOR LIFE ON ALL LEVELS, ALTHOUGH ITS CAUTIOUS ATTITUDE CAN SOMETIMES MASK THIS. BUT THEN **CONTRADICTIONS** TEND TO RUN IN YOUR PET'S NATURE. IT CAN BE FULL OF PURRS AND LOVE ONE MINUTE, THEN HAUGHTY AND DISTANT THE NEXT; CONFIDENT AND OUTGOING FROM AFAR, THEN SWINGING TO **SHY**, **SENSITIVE** AND **WITHDRAWN** UPON APPROACH; HAPPY AND MERRY IN ATTITUDE, THEN SWITCHING TO **MOODY** AND **PRE-OCCUPIED**. WHEN A CAPRICORN CAT IS LIKE THIS, IT IS BECAUSE IT IS LIVING TOO MUCH IN THE PAST.

The Capricorn cat is ruled by Saturn, god of time, duty, karma and preservation. When you call your star puss, it will usually be pretty prompt in obeying because it knows you have something to do together.

Your pet is appreciative that you are making this attempt to secure more information about it. Your Capricorn cat is of the opinion that this is "actually a superior way to uncover its personality" and also helps to settle its slight insecurity (not observable, of course) that you may not be aware of its "passionate conviction" about the importance of your relationship as cat and person. Now that more of its character structure can be made clear, your star cat feels this will "work to improve the quality" of your already good partnership. Your feline murmurs, "But I am ambitious, and always aim to make it better."

In a way Catus capricornicus is the classic cat, and you are likely to have a classic cat–person relationship relative to your situation. For example, if the Capricorn feline is a mouser on the farm, then that is what it is. And it is bound to be pretty good at it, too, in its desire to please you. If you are a Very Important Person, then this star creature is almost without exception a most dignified, noble and correctly behaved cat. Your cat whispers to me that it's "sure you understand" what I'm trying to convey. Catus capricornicus can fill the whole spectrum of cat vocations, although it has some reservations when it comes to a New Age pet–owner relationship. Your puss wants to elaborate: "For instance, if you were a rock star, made loud noises, kept unpredictable hours and expected me to do likewise, I don't think I would really enjoy that situation. It's probably more suited to a Sagittarius or Aquarius cat. But if it was for you, and you loved me and wanted me, I'd give it a darn good try." What an animal! So just to recap, this is a cat that will work to create the most out of any traditional and **orthodox** cat–person situation.

The Capricorn cat looks to its owner for status and protection and can be extremely good at organizing its environment when it has both in good measure. Being loyal and dedicated to you, this star puss takes its responsibility as your cat seriously. This feline is highly purposeful and works for practical results from any activity. Catus capricornicus wants to voice an opinion: "It should be constitutionally written that all prime ministers and presidents own a Capricorn cat since we can embody organizational ability and skill in crisis management, not to mention efficient use of time. We are particularly good at structure. Plus we do succeed—finally. I'm with you, am I not? That indicates something of what I mean. We are winners in the long term." Thank you, Capricorn cat.

This star cat has a large appetite for life on all levels, although its cautious attitude can sometimes mask this. But then contradictions tend to run in your pet's nature, as you have probably observed. It can be full of purrs and love one minute, then haughty and distant the next; confident and outgoing from afar, then swinging to shy, sensitive and withdrawn upon approach; happy and merry in attitude, then switching to moody and preoccupied. When a Capricorn cat is very much like this it is because it is living too much in the past via the legendary Capricornian memory, and probably brooding over incidents long forgotten! The best strategy to adopt in these cases is just to give lots of love and acceptance. Make it verbally known if the cat won't accept cuddles. Then it will soon grow out of it. Your cat pipes up: "But **I'm** definitely not turning into an Edgar Allen Poe (yes, he was a Capricorn) sort of a cat. I just act like this to keep you on your toes."

Gosh! See what a wise and wily cat you've got? But Capricorn cats also have a certain charisma. (Your puss is whispering to me again: "As a human, Elvis Presley embodied this quality well.") And they are **very** determined. With this pussikins it's definitely a matter of if at first you don't succeed, try again and again, maybe using another method. Your puss murmurs: "We have been known to resort to sneaky tactics now and then." This cat gets what it wants— eventually. ("Long-term winners, remember?" says your cat.) Yet this feline is not a risk taker. The only time Capricorn felines **ever** take a gamble is after having thoroughly calculated the outcome.

Their sensible and practical qualities combined with their determination serve to ensure a high degree of success. But the Capricorn cat doesn't muster its resources just to gain its own ends; it will employ its strength in your causes, too. In whatever part of the spectrum the Capricorn cat and its owner find themselves, from mouser cat and owner to VIP and pet, it will put its force behind you whenever possible. Most of the time you know nothing about it. Your cat murmurs: "Perhaps it's better when you don't."

Your star cat hopes you realize just how important you are to it and the construction of its world. This puss is probably going to be around for a while. Whether or not they are robust as kittens, upon reaching maturity Capricorn animals tend to live for a long time, so it's best you understand how, whether observed or not, your pussikins orients most of its life around you. Maybe you've noticed something of this in the way that your pet will often seek you out, just to find out what you are up to. It does a little patrol in order to check up on things.

Obviously this cat functions best in a reasonably ordered routine—mealtimes at predictable hours, with life around it flowing reasonably smoothly. The Capricorn cat can get awfully confused by disorder and disruption. Your pet has something to add: "Particularly when no attention is paid to my well-being. In these instances I have been known to do something that you regard as naughty, but all I'm attempting to do is indicate my state of mind." Yes. Quite so. Normally this is an obedient cat that pays attention to your wishes.

In some ways Capricorns are knowing animals. There can be occasions where you see a flash of something in them that goes beyond your daily cat. An ancient wisdom is in their eyes. Your feline wants me to write: "It's there for you." But Capricorns are also funny cats when the mood takes them. They can be as hilarious as the Marx brothers, and then again as proper as Emily Post, as glamorous as Marlene Dietrich and as psychic as Jeane Dixon. (Your star pet wagers that "the cats belonging to these Capricorn icons would all be like that, too!") All these qualities and more are what your Capricorn creature brings to your first-class cat–person relationship.

This star puss identifies with the home situation, and if the truth be known, is actually a little snooty about it. Whatever your situation together, it's blue ribbon to your cat, which adds: "Call me a snob if you like, but I always select the best." So there you have it, esteemed, revered and beloved owner, the inside story on your cat, which is dedicated to your causes eternally.

It's a complex, sensitive and clever cat, this one. Your pet has been rather straightforward with you on the qualities it possesses. Look after this cat and you have a great pet, beyond price. Its training in the temple of Sophia, the ancient Greek goddess of wisdom, still stands it in very good stead. Make certain to give your felicitous feline good amounts of whole milk to keep the bones and teeth strong. Also, if you haven't already done so, try the animal on dry food. Capricorn cats can love to crunch on biscuits.

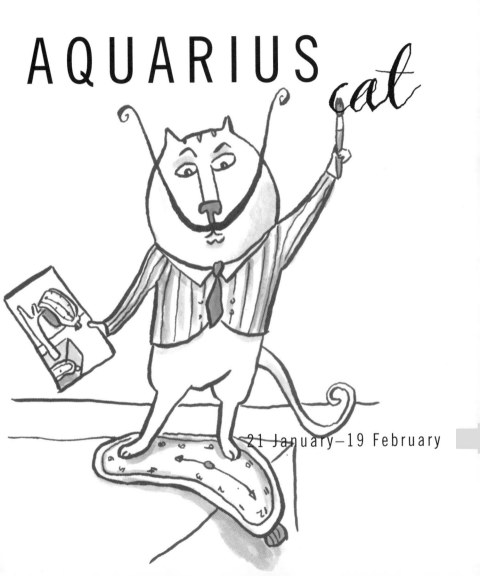

**herb:** Elderberry

**stone:** Amethyst

**number:** 4

**element:** Air—watches for spacecraft at night

**celebrity cat:** Sizi—Albert Einstein's cat

IT CAN BE TAKEN FOR GRANTED THAT THIS IS AN **UNUSUAL** ANIMAL. BECAUSE OF THE GREAT URGE AN AQUARIAN CREATURE IS BORN WITH FOR FREEDOM AND EXPRESSION OF ITS UNIQUE SPIRIT, COMPROMISE AND CONFORMITY DON'T COME EASY TO THIS MEMBER OF THE ZODIAC. YOUR CAT INTERJECTS: "I AM WHAT I AM. LIKE IT OR NOT, I HAVE TO BE ME." THIS CAN MANIFEST AS MOST **UNCONVENTIONAL** FELINE BEHAVIOR. AS A MINOR EXAMPLE, THIS PUSS MIGHT PREFER DOG FOOD TO CAT FOOD. (ONE AQUARIAN CAT IN MY ACQUAINTANCE EVEN USED TO EAT LETTUCE AND TOMATO ON RYE!)

**T**he Aquarius cat is ruled by Uranus, god of freedom, genius, technology and eccentricity. When it is called, this star cat can appear lightning quick, especially when it knows something interesting is in the air.

Your cat thinks it superb that you have managed to lay hands on this astro-profile about it. It considers this "definitely a good way to increase our understanding," and "appropriate," because your feline's sign has a natural affinity with astrology. You will obtain more insight into your Aquarius cat's nature, and what you may currently regard as quirks will be seen for what they really are—as your puss puts it, "part and parcel of a totally unique animal that follows its own rules." It feels that your cat–person bond can only benefit as you become aware that: "We have a very special thing going." Well, that's clear enough.

It can be taken for granted that this is an unusual animal. Because of the great urge an Aquarian creature is born with for freedom and expression of its unique spirit, compromise and conformity don't come easy to this member of the Zodiac. Your cat interjects: "I am what I am. Like it or not, I have to be me." This can manifest as most unconventional feline behavior. As a minor example, this puss might prefer dog food to cat food. (One Aquarian cat in my acquaintance even used to eat lettuce and tomato on rye!) Another example is that Aquarians are the sort of cats that **love** to go in the car. (It is a fact that the odd well-placed Aquarian kitty has enjoyed traveling in its human's private jet.) There are some Aquarian cats that come across as being fairly normal. But you can be sure that if you look hard enough or scratch deep enough ("Intelligent pun," quips your cat), a strong streak of difference will be found. Each Aquarian cat has an individual personality with some odd ways, even if it is only playing the role of the average cat to perfection. "Now that is quirky!" says your cat.

Even though your feline may appear aloof at times, it truly cares for you very much. But this is an unpossessive animal (well, mostly anyway), and so tends not to make lavish demands for affection from you. (Neither does it expect high demands from you.) Also, being a strong believer in equality (the French Revolution was an Aquarian event), this star cat has difficulty in buying into the docile pet and owner situation, preferring instead to see you as a friend. Your cat's itching to have its say: "Certainly you are the most **important** individual in my life and I have a great love of you. But my own nature is so strong that I can't subjugate my personality to others' perception of me." Fortunately Catus aquarius is usually found with a special person—"Like you!" beams your cat—who understands its needs well because they have similar sorts of inclinations themselves! And often you will share a home and lifestyle that's unusual and different. But even when the situation appears fairly normal, you can be sure, unique person, that you and your cat have some special reason for being together. It may not flash out like a fluorescent light immediately, but there is a deeper meaning to you and your Aquarian star cat's association on the planet. But don't worry because you can be sure time will tell.

Being intelligent this puss knows what it likes and what it doesn't. It's unlikely to be terribly food fussy. The Aquarian cat will either eat something (whatever it is!) or it won't. This feline is hungry for life and experience generally. Now your pet's usurping the pen! "So you don't have to worry about **me** starving to death! Also, I recharge my energies through sleep so you will find me alert on waking. During observation my eyes are always rather piercing and all-seeing; however, upon return from the electric lands I visit, they can have the force of lightning." [The cosmic serpent on the Egyptian Pharaoh's forehead was supposed to symbolize this quality of Aquarius—*Author*.] "Sun and fire re-energize me, too."

Now the pen's been returned, I can continue with the narrative. Generally your cat likes your friends and is courteous when they are visiting. But this star puss is inquisitive and experimental, too. So if it wants to check or test the person out, it will do so without much hesitation. This puss is capable of doing unpredictable things. ("Perhaps that could be a warning for the unwary," quietly suggests your cat.) Catus aquarius takes pleasure in positive interaction so it enjoys seeing you with your friends, particularly if you are gathered for some worthwhile activity. Your pet puts forward some examples: "Like a Mensa meeting, a consciousness-raising endeavor, a New Age project, or just a great happy party where everyone is themselves!" There may be one or two visitors to the house that the cat takes a particular shine to (there may be one or two that it particularly dislikes, too), and it makes that quite obvious. They might be completely unlikely and disparate people as well. Actually this cat could have some animal friends of its own. Being especially tolerant, this feline can get along with most creatures if it so wishes. For instance, it's quite within the bounds of probability that this puss will swap ideas with a possum or a bandicoot. One well-fed Aquarian cat in recent history even got along with the household bird!

Although Aquarians are group-conscious animals, they do need their own space—often. You will see them go off by themselves just to find a quiet place where they can contemplate. "I need time to consider life," the cat explains. Actually, it is best to respect this need and not allow the creature to be bothered or followed at such times. The cat wants to give more details about its need for solitude: "Because I have a special talent in regards to tuning into cosmic energy and through this can energize your true wishes, and empower the unfolding of our life in general." Wow!

This is a strong cat. Some Aquarius kitties may give the impression of fragility but they are usually as tough as old boots underneath. Aquarius cats have a great hold on life and can be as long-lived as the Capricorn creatures. The cat's taking up the pen again! "We can be possessed of incredible determination, too. Once I know what I want, I usually get it. And when I'm in top form I focus this ability into your causes as well. I am capable of attracting abrupt change." [The "hundredth monkey" was probably an Aquarian—*Author.*] "Take reasonable care of me and I'll live up to my responsibilities to you. Look after me and I'll look after you.

"Some final words: children and myself get along reasonably well, but not when there's any tail pulling. When it gets too ridiculous, I'll just quit the scene. Actually, that applies to everything. Those times when things get on my nerves I'll simply disappear. But I'll always come back to you, beloved owner, because we have some interesting and special times in store."

With pen (finally!) back in hand, I'm able to say that Aquarian cats can at times seem to have the mentality of a human. But they are all cat as well. This makes them dynamic and interesting creatures, full of potential for development. This futuristic feline is associated with the not widely available 1964 Aquarian tarot deck, dictated from space by a being called "one" to a group on Earth for the New Age. The cat's creative fire is particularly linked with the classical figure of "Hierophant," keeper of the keys to the secrets, who becomes "The Speaker" in the 1964 tarot. That card is depicted with lightning bolts and fiery energy, showing that the knowledge is being put out there for everyone—multiple-level communication that can no longer be locked away. Perceive and delight in your cat's individuality and you will be rewarded with a fascinating and entertaining companion. Just don't let your cat get close to any faulty electrical equipment.

# PISCES
## *cat*

20 February–20 March

**herb:** Bilberry

**stone:** Moonstone

**number:** 12

**element:** Water—talks with the angels

**celebrity cat:** Fluffy—Eric Cartman's cat in *South Park*

AN UNKIND WORD—EVEN AN UNKIND LOOK!—CAN MAKE
**CATUS PISCES** MISERABLE FOR SOME TIME. IT WILL GO OFF
IN HURT AND **CONFUSION** AND **BROOD** ON WHAT HAPPENED.
IF FOR ANY REASON THIS GOES ON FOR TOO LONG, THIS
FELINE CAN BECOME ILL, CERTAINLY LISTLESS AND
LACKLUSTER. BUT BEING EXTREMELY **SENSITIVE** TO BOTH
NEGATIVE AND POSITIVE VIBRATIONS MEANS THAT IF THIS
IS EVER THE CASE, ALL YOU HAVE TO DO IS GIVE YOUR
PISCES PUSS LOTS OF LOVE, **CARE**, **ATTENTION** AND
SOOTHING.

**T**he Pisces cat is ruled by Neptune, god of images, illusions, movies, mysticism and universal love. When you call your cat it will appear—sometimes sooner, sometimes later, depending on its emotions—because your puss knows that really you do love it.

Your star cat is eager to say: "Thank you, beautiful person, for having this astrological perspective on me delivered into your hands. This way you will find things about me, **your** pet, that you may not otherwise know. Your further understanding of my sometimes mysterious personality will serve to enrich our interaction together. And I will be better able to express myself and my eternal feelings for you. Our relationship will become even more delightful."

Well, your pet is happy to have that off its chest. But it must be said at the beginning that Catus pisces, as your cat, feels a very strong bond with you. Your pet urgently desires the pen again: "My karma is to be with you, and I am bound to you by a great love. Ours is an infinitely special relationship." [The Pope's cat has to be a Pisces—*Author.*] "My devotion to you is pivotal to my life." [It's so strong, you may even see your puss in your dreams!—*Author.*] However, the depth of this star cat's feelings can make it vulnerable and easily hurt. An unkind word—even an unkind look!—can make Catus pisces miserable for some time. It will go off in hurt and confusion and brood on what happened. If for any reason this goes on for too long this feline can become ill, certainly listless and lackluster. But being extremely sensitive to both negative and **positive** vibrations means that if this is ever the case—"And I can be over-sensitive, thus can be acting this way for reasons unknown by you," your cat earnestly clarifies—all you have to do is give your Pisces puss lots of love, care, attention and soothing. "Yes," says your pet, "then soon my rainbow spirits rise again and life is wondrous once more."

Obviously your cat is more than a little receptive to your moods and state of being. It takes a lot of its cues from you and is **utterly** dependent on how you are. Having a high degree of intuition your Piscean kitty is usually able to sense what is happening for you and can often silently appear when you need it. However, when this star cat is in a situation where its emotions and happiness are continually scrambled—subjected to continual teasing, a harsh insensitive owner, and that sort of thing—its intuitive abilities never become accessible to it but remain caught in confusion. Your cat's bursting to have another say: "Fortunately, that doesn't happen to me. I am with **you**, my rightful and beloved owner. You would **never** allow me to be subject to such shabby treatment. Our wonderful experience together will continue to grow and unfold in a world of happiness."

One has to believe in dreams to have them come true. And this cat is a great believer in dreams. When the Piscean kitty is in a loving, wholesome situation, it can make those dreams come true, too. A developed Pisces cat has high spiritual strength and not inconsiderable psychic powers. "However," your puss wants to make clear, "we must never be used for nefarious gain. It will always backfire," adding: "Scorpio cat knows all about the disastrous consequences following misuse of occult energy." It is best to just allow your pet to be brimful with life's magic; it then flows in the new days that continually dawn. Because your creature's love is so focused on you, it serves as a channel (when all is well) that good things can come through. So simply allow your Pisces feline its funny little ways—gazing at rain through the window, watching the clouds move, seeking rainbows, and generally softly padding around chasing the tail of forever. At times your poetic pet can seem lost in its own world. But it maintains that it's "just preoccupied in discovering an elusive vision within."

Nice food gives the Pisces puss pleasure. It does enjoy the odd special delicacy, and can do well on fish. Its saucer of milk needs to be always available because it likes to lap at it on and off through the day. Sleep of course is of great importance to this star pet. It has the pen and is off again! "Not only does my body rest and refresh itself, but I travel the realms of mystery, replenishing my soul and paying homage to the creative forces of life. My aura is always subtly but potently charged when I return. This boosts my healing abilities, too." Well said, and true! In fact, before medical technology became so effective, a Pisces cat was often to be seen by sick beds in an effort to draw upon this healing power. There is much compassion and self-sacrifice in evolved Piscean animals. Actually they probably comprised the majority of the animals recently used in studies with the depressed, the mentally disturbed and otherwise institutionalized people—studies with extremely good results, too, it hardly seems necessary to add.

Your star pet loves to snuggle up to you in a warm bed, or sit with you by a fire. Cuddles are something this puss really enjoys. The Piscean creature instinctively likes nature and will wander the garden on its voyages. "Sometimes passing the time with the fairies who live there," your pet chimes in. If the Pisces cat lives near the sea with its owner, it's extremely fulfilled since it has a strong affinity with the ocean and will sit on a high peak to watch it. As with Sagittarius cat, the Pisces cat can enjoy all types of music. Sometimes it will even be a TV or video viewer! The Pisces puss is highly receptive to color and beauty and is a bit of a romantic at heart.

The harmony of everyday life together is extremely important to your feline. The cat's desperate for a say now: "Our home and household is enshrined in my heart, just below you. I'm actually quite sentimental in what I feel, although you might only see this indirectly, perhaps observing this in my luminous eyes as I regard everybody at the dinner table. You probably think I'm just on the scrounge for a tidbit (well, that too; I ask nicely in my musical tones, do I not?), but it's more that I'm feeling a great surge of love in my heart. I'm just so **glad** to be with you. Not like one of those poor mistreated Pisces cats that just couldn't take the agony of their situation any more and slipped away into the night, seeking another fate." As your pet ponders this cruel enormity, I'm able to reclaim the pen. But, yes, right, in unhappy circumstances a Pisces cat will do that—simply vanish, never to be seen again. This is to be observed that many defectors belong to the sign of Pisces.

Numerous people involved with the arts are Piscean, for example, Rudolph Nureyev, Kiri Te Kanawa, George Harrison and Elizabeth Taylor. "This quality of creativity extends to me, and together we can create a truly special relationship," writes your cat with the deftly stolen pen. "You only have to love me and be kind to me."

Well, fair enough. Catus pisces did indeed have something
to say. A Piscean cat can be one of the most beautiful and
gentle creatures on earth, shedding subtle magic as it
moves through life. There are definitely special qualities
to these cats, probably gathered and perfected when they
attended Hapy, the god of the Nile, a most important
member of the ancient Egyptian pantheon indeed.
However, as your pet has softly insisted, kindness and love
are prerequisites to this cat unfolding to its full potential.
Also, never leave traps or other foot-capturing contrivances
around, as these are special dangers for Pisces puss.

# ZODIAC *cat* OWNERS

 (usually called "humans")

# ARIES OWNER

This owner is an "instant action" person. And one with a short fuse. As a kitten you'll get some leeway as you learn the ropes, but you'd better learn them fast. Too many lapses in the kitty litter department and you could be picked up by the scruff of your neck and hurled out the door. And when your owner says, "Come here, cat," or "Cat, let go of the bird," or whatever, you **must** obey at once. Otherwise it could be "Stupid cat," and you're handed on to someone else. But are you also capable of exhibiting exceptional behavior? I'm referring to things like standing up to the dog; alerting your owner to a ringing telephone or a fire; or accompanying your owner to soccer, tennis or other outside activities. Are you an independent spirit, a confident—rather than needy—cat, able to cope with unpredictability? Like when your Aries owner gets caught up in the latest enthusiasm and consequently your dinner's late. Possibly you're expected to fend for yourself in these instances—catch a mouse or work the self-feeding device. Yes? Then you've found your owner and you're in for an adventurous life. Together you'll form a mutual admiration society because of the qualities you share. And you'll get plenty of red meat because your owner figures, "A real cat deserves real food."

**TIP:** Always be fiercely loyal to your owner.

**ARIEN OWNERS:** Spike Milligan; Joan Crawford; Marlon Brando; Aretha Franklin; Vincent van Gogh; Emma Thompson.

## TAURUS OWNER

Predictability is what you are blessed with here—especially pertaining to mealtimes—that is, provided you behave yourself in accordance with your Taurean owner's expectations. You'll receive lots of loving care and attention when you're a kitten, and a certain amount of furniture scratching, pot plant uprooting or other misdemeanors will be put up with in the name of your growing up. However, when you're an adult you'd better respect the comfy home you and your owner share. It may seem that you're getting away with naughty escapades relatively lightly, but be warned, once you've crossed the line—and **all** Taureans have a line—there will be a change in attitude. You're likely to find yourself promptly put outside in the cold after minor misbehaviors. Wheedling by the fridge door won't produce the usual treats. In fact, it may not even be tolerated. Nevertheless, by being a wise and loving cat and practicing full-throated purring, you'll be a prized and **treasured** member of the family. And you'll be given full benefits, which in the warm and affectionate Taurean nature are ample and plentiful.

**TIP:** Meow musically, and always greet your owner with sinuous leg rubbing.

**TAUREAN OWNERS:** William Shakespeare; Dame Nellie Melba; Benjamin Spock; Cher; Jerry Seinfeld; Candice Bergman.

# GEMINI OWNER

If you're after an interesting life and fancy the idea of being spoken to as an equal, then it could be a Gemini owner for you. However, can you understand and will you be able to communicate back? This is **essential**. Remember, you will have to be clever and up to speed with your owner's train of thought—which, I must warn you, can move incredibly fast. If you still think you're up to it, be the kitten that stares quizzically yet intently at this potential owner. It helps if you're cute, too. After negotiating conditions, your Gemini owner will zoom home with you and expect you to behave yourself in the car. From that point on, the less of a nuisance you are and the more you delight and amuse them, the more successfully you and your owner will bond. Your owner is likely to have lots of friends, and you must be polite and conduct yourself intelligently to hold up your end of the cat–person relationship. You must also be quiet and understanding if they are writing or on the phone—**no** yowling for attention and ruining their concentration. In return, your owner will treat you as a true friend. You will hear their confidences, their theories and their creative plans. Your opinion will be sought, even your help. And you will have a wonderful time being plied with the best new cat food and the latest in feline products. Curled on your owner's lap, sharing thoughts as they read, you will purr with deep and happy satisfaction at your lot in life.

**TIP:** Perfect your ESP.

**GEMINIAN OWNERS:** Queen Victoria; Frank Lloyd Wright; Naomi Campbell; Paul McCartney; Wallis Simpson; Miles Davis.


# CANCER OWNER

If you long for security, a place you know you can call home, with meals arriving at regular times, then this may well be the owner for you. However, you must be willing to be fussed over. This doesn't mean all the time, but when the Cancerian owner wants attention, its pet had better be ready to respond. It may be that they want to see how the color of the blanket they're knitting you looks next to your fur, or they might want to hold you close and sob all their misery into your warm and understanding ear. It could be anything really. The Cancerian owner can be rather dramatic as well as emotionally sensitive and sometimes rather bossy. You may be called into the room to prove a point; perhaps something along the lines of, "See! The cat cares for me more than you do!" That kind of thing. You must learn how to read your owner's moods. Being **sympatico** will make life infinitely better for both you and your owner. You'll sit under the night sky and watch the moon rise together. You'll happily sit in the kitchen as your owner bustles about preparing you some fabulous food on an up day. You'll sit on their knee purring, imparting love and positive power on a down day. And your owner will never part with **you**, the one being that "truly understands" them.

**TIP:** Don't make too much of a fuss over other people.

**CANCERIAN OWNERS:** Gough Whitlam; Barbara Cartland; Mike Tyson; Ruth Cracknell; Tom Cruise; Kathy Bates.

## LEO OWNER

Do you think you look good? (You don't actually have to be a purebred. You can even get away with a crumpled ear and eyes that don't match. But you must have an **unshakable** belief in your superiority and invincibility, which surrounds you in a golden aura.) Do you think you can be amusing yet cut the moment (when necessary) with haughty and regal disdain? But, and this is probably the most important qualification of all, are you capable of great love and devotion? If you've answered "yes" to all these, then you and the Leo owner are made for each other. The Leo owner already has feline affinity in their soul, their Sign being associated with the lion (a.k.a. the "king of the jungle") as it is. To catch their eye, look at them with head erect, very knowingly, and project solid-gold "class" unwaveringly. The Leo owner will recognize you as a kindred spirit and will want to take you home **at once**! And a good life you're in for, too. This warm-hearted owner will tend you well as a kitten, and be a wonderful companion when you're an adult. If you're a pedigree (or perhaps even if you're not) it's likely you'll spend a lot of time at cat shows. (It's best to win, too.) Even if you don't, you should make sure that you adorn the ottoman most regally, making sure all your owner's friends gasp at "what a wonderful cat" you are. When you and your owner comfortably stare into the fire together on a cold winter's night, it will be with the knowledge that two stars of the universe have found each other.

**TIP:** Always share the limelight with your owner.

**LEONINE OWNERS:** The Queen Mother; Mick Jagger; Madonna; Cecil B. de Mille; Alexander the Great; Coco Chanel.


## VIRGO OWNER

There's a lot of cat in the Virgoan owner's spirit. They are neat, clean and fastidious in an exceptionally feline way, and they don't lack style, either. This probably comes from past lives in which they performed duties in the temple of Bastet—the ancient Egyptian cat goddess of fertility and good health, also known as "Pasht"—where it is said the word "puss" comes from. (But you'd know more about that than me.) On the other hand, they can have an inner tussle between superiority and inferiority (also stemming from Bastet days, where they had to get the balance right or whammo!—no over-stepping the line in this powerful goddess' service), causing them to shun the spotlight. Are you still with me, and are you still interested? Good. Because it's very important to understand the **psychology** of the Virgoan owner in order to bond successfully. And let me tell you, life with a Virgoan owner can be as good as it gets for a cat. All their service to Bastet still runs in their veins. Feel your way with this owner. They can be quite psychic, draw on your intuition to feel your way in. And do make sure you're glistening and well washed. Maybe decorously walk over and quietly sit at their feet, perhaps giving a delicate sneeze. You would have charmed them by your approach then alarmed them by your sneeze. You—"poor little thing"—will be collected up to be taken home and looked after. And thus will be your days thereafter, but even better if you repay your owner with warm love and appreciation of their inner selves.

**TIP:** Make sure your owner knows you're aware of your special bond.

**VIRGOAN OWNERS:** Van Morrison; Queen Elizabeth I; Sir Donald Bradman; Sophia Loren; Brian Henderson; Cameron Diaz.

# LIBRAN OWNER

See that person with a confident tilt of the head, the stylish presentation and the fabulous dress sense? That is a Libran owner. Now, if you desire a Libran owner you are going to have to be pretty much that way, too. The Libran owner can be kind and caring, but not endlessly. Wimps and wusses had best look elsewhere for a human. Those of you still in obviously think you have what it takes. OK. Could you take to wearing a diamond collar? Good. Do you look fabulous on a velvet ottoman or a faux zebra skin sofa? Are you willing to obey your owner's wishes, but at the same time have a mind of your own? Can you be courteous and charming when your owner is entertaining? If you're answering "yes," then the signs are good. But your owner will demand **total** love and **adoration** from you. Displays of clever, independent behavior are allowed, though heaven help you if you display more affection for another human or, perhaps worse, scratch up the Louis XIV furniture! Nevertheless, if you're up to all this, you'll get very much the same treatment in return, as well as having excellent care taken of you. So polish your claws, clean your coat, sit nice and straight and look **gorgeous** to snare your Libran owner.

**TIP:** Never disgrace yourself in public in any way whatsoever.

**LIBRAN OWNERS:** Olivia Newton-John; George Gershwin; Katherine Mansfield; Roger Moore; Heather Locklear; Sir Cliff Richard.


## SCORPIO OWNER

If you're a cat who can remember lifetimes in the service of Osiris (ancient Egyptian god, supreme judge and ruler of the afterworld) or Merlin, assisting in mighty magic, or if you have flown on a broomstick or two you may do well to consider the Scorpio owner. You're obviously a cat who can handle the power of the occult and can thrive at the cutting edge of creation. The Pluto-ruled Scorpion has deep affinity with these things, and this owner's intense, magnetic nature not only probes the mysteries, but also draws these to them. And you, of course, can be of great help when your Scorpio owner feels invisible forces gathering and whispering past their ears, or is delving into the depths of Nature's secrets. They are driven to **find out**, to go behind the veils behind the veils. You must signal your mastery here. You don't have to be black (although that does immediately engage their attention) but you must have a powerfully concentrated aura.

As magic is the art of timing, you must choose exactly the right moment to impress yourself upon this owner's consciousness. Perhaps putting your paw on their hand as they tentatively pat you, or following them as they leave (I'm sure you can work this out better than me)—something like that. You'll be regarded intently. Stare just as intently back. Swiftly and silently you'll be swept up, as the destiny that has brought you into each other's orbit cements the wonderful and meaningful path you will walk together, and your owner allows you into the inner sanctum of their soul.

**TIP:** Never let your owner stray onto the wrong path.

**SCORPIO OWNERS:** Prince Charles; Jodie Foster; Captain James Cook; Joan Sutherland; Feodor Dostoevsky; Marie Antoinette.

## SAGITTARIAN OWNER

If you are an easygoing cat, one with a philosophical yet robust and happy nature, you and the Sagittarian owner could be the perfect match. Mind you, be very aware, you're probably going to need every one of your nine lives. It's not so much that this owner will knowingly endanger you (that's the furthest thing from their minds), but far more the case that their lives are jam-packed with activities and adventures, some amazing kinds, and you are expected to keep up. Sagittarian owners have been known to take their cat surfing or riding pillion on their motorbike, or get them working the ropes on the yacht. And you must absolutely **love** inclusion in all these pursuits on which your owner takes you. The Sagittarian owner tires quickly of a cat possessed of few interests. However, you two would probably spot each other pretty quickly, and **know** at once that you were meant to be together, as like reflects like. It would be an **instant** thing, and off you'd go in their arms into a brave New World, chasing marvelous horizons of ever-expanding opportunities. You'd listen as they played awesome music, perhaps chipping in here and there. You'd hear their plans for corporate takeovers, nodding sagely now and then while the Lear jet was being refueled. You'd jump up and run outside with them towards the rainbow that arched over the next valley of promise.

**TIP:** Be companionable and accepting of your owner's friends.

**SAGITTARIAN OWNERS:** Mark Twain; Tina Turner; Ludwig van Beethoven; Maria Callas; Jimi Hendrix; John Paul Getty.


# CAPRICORN OWNER

Do you care for a structured life, one where time is planned purposefully? Are you willing and able to make yourself useful to this owner? Would you, for example: catch mice that are making a nuisance of themselves; remind your owner of important appointments; enhance your owner's prestige by being an incredibly impressive cat; and, perhaps most importantly, be able to lift your owner's spirits when they sag under the apparent futility of it all. If you have the high level of organizational ability that a serious life involves and you believe that ambitious effort is a prerequisite to producing anything, yet you can also lighten up and look on the bright side when life's corridors appear to darken, you will be **indispensable** to the Capricorn owner. They are often corporate high flyers, involved in government or other highly responsible positions, and although extremely efficient, at times they can come perilously close to succumbing to their own negative criticisms. This is when you must step in and project the love that heals their feelings of inadequacy, guilt or whatever. If you can combine these two factors of dutifulness and dedication you were ordained for a Capricorn owner. So smarten up, look like a sensible but not unfeeling cat, and kismet will guide your Capricorn owner to you. In quiet delight they will carry you home, so together you can become a winning team.

**TIP:** Never make an exhibition of yourself.

**CAPRICORN OWNERS:** Mel Gibson; Joan of Arc; Muhammad Ali; Marianne Faithfull; Elvis Presley; Maggie Smith.

# AQUARIUS OWNER

This owner is acutely aware that there are more things under the Sun than Horatio ever dreamed of, to paraphrase the great bard. And you must be, too, to successfully connect with the Aquarian owner. No commonplace, dull cat of little brain would suit this owner. It must be a cat in tune with the cosmic mind, able to intuit the greater picture on the world stage (Shakespeare had Aquarius rising), capable of making the quantum leap to the next evolutionary step, and have an interest in unexplained phenomena, such as UFOs or what happens in the Bermuda Triangle. If you are excited by the thought of a constantly expanding world and constructive colonization of cyberspace, then you and the Aquarian owner have a great future together. But forget it if you're an insecure and needy cat or can't take to unorthodox and unusual meals. For those of you still with me, do you consider that you are a unique and **original** being, capable of matching the Aquarian owner's individual but unpredictable spirit? Then what are you waiting for? Telepath into space that you are now ready for your owner. Synchronicity will bring you together, as the cosmos oversees your meeting of minds and the fulfillment of your special destiny together.

**TIP:** Surprise your owner with a few well-engineered "coincidences."

**AQUARIAN OWNERS:** Charles Dickens; Dame Edna Everage; Galileo; Vanessa Redgrave; Thomas Edison; Cybill Shepherd.

# PISCES OWNER

If you are looking for an owner with vast depth of feeling, one that can have an instinctive grasp of soul power and psychically sense the stock market or when the angels are near, then look no further. The Piscean owner will share your dreams, may even travel with you sometimes in the astral realms, and, like you, is able to hear the heavenly strains of the universal choir in creation. But some will disguise this great sensitivity behind a hard-headed mask and become extremely successful in the business world. So you have to discern which Piscean person you want—whether natural-born New Age mystic or strategic master of the markets.

The first type you would appeal to through meaningful communion, the latter through savvy eye contact. However, with either of them, you will have to be a great transmitter of the divinity and interrelatedness of all life because even the apparently skeptical Pisces owner is sensitive to this, deep down, and both types of Piscean will **expect** this of you. You would need to operate as a channel, a conduit, of spiritual energy and power, linking the earthly and angelic realms. The cat–person bond between you will be strung with the stars of both worlds, as you walk the special avenue of meaning that has been marked out for you to share.

**TIP:** Always have your act together.

**PISCEAN OWNERS:** Edgar Cayce; Jean Harlow; Albert Einstein; Glenn Close; Michelangelo; Sharon Stone.

**Helen Hope**, a well-respected and internationally known astrologer, grew up in a conservative community in New Zealand before going to college in Australia. She studied sociology, anthropology and mathematics at Victoria and Auckland University; however, it was during the three years she lived in Singapore and took time to read the collected works of Carl Jung that she was turned on to astrology. She returned to New Zealand and took intensive, formal training in astrology. Helen now writes regular astrology columns for two magazines—*New Ideas* and *She*. She lives in Australia.